MASTER

YOUR

WEALTH

USING 21 PROVEN LAWS

by

SHAILAJA SHEKHAR

WHY IS THIS BOOK FOR YOU?

- **Transformative Journey from Financial Struggle to Prosperity:**

Imagine if you're always worried about money, barely making ends meet. This book promises to guide you on a path that will change this situation. It's like a roadmap for going from financial stress to a place where you feel more comfortable and secure with your money.

- **Tired of Living Paycheck to Paycheck:**

If you feel like you're always just getting by with your income and you want things to be better, this book understands that struggle. It's designed to help you break free from that cycle of barely having enough money to cover your expenses.

- **More Than Just Wealth Building:**

This book isn't only about teaching you how to accumulate money. It's much more than that. It's like a source of motivation and encouragement, pushing you to believe that there's a lot of opportunity for you to have more in your life, not just financially, but in terms of overall well-being and satisfaction.

- **Prosperity without Harming Others or the Environment:**

Sometimes, people think that to become wealthy, you have to take advantage of others or exploit natural resources. This book challenges that idea. It believes that you can achieve prosperity while still being fair to others and being mindful of the environment.

- **A Fresh Perspective and Sustained Action:**

This book suggests that in order to change your financial situation, you need to look at things from a new angle. It encourages you to commit to making continuous efforts over time. It's not just a one-time fix, but a shift in mindset and a series of actions that you consistently take.

- **Cultivating a Wealth-Oriented Mindset:**

Think of your mindset as the way you think about money and wealth. This book will teach you how to adopt a mindset that's geared towards building and maintaining wealth. It's like training your brain to think in a way that leads to financial success.

- **Steps to Manifest Your Financial Dreams:**

It's one thing to have dreams about what you want your financial situation to be like, but it's another to turn those dreams into reality. This book promises to provide you with clear, practical steps that you can follow to make your financial aspirations come true.

In simpler terms, this book is like a friendly guide that helps you move from struggling with money to feeling more comfortable and secure. It understands the challenges of living paycheck to paycheck and offers both motivation and practical advice. It also emphasizes that you can achieve financial success without harming others or the environment, and it teaches you how to think and act in a way that leads to wealth. Finally, it gives you clear steps to turn your financial dreams into actual achievements.

TABLE OF CONTENTS

INTRODUCTION

This is not an intellectual book; rather, the emphasis is on the practical application of the material presented. This is not a theoretical treatise; rather, it is a guide for practitioners that includes both theoretical and practical information.

This book is aimed at people who want to become affluent first and then consider what it all means afterward; these people are the target audience for the book. It is written for both men and women who have an immediate need for money and is directed at those needs.

Those who have not had the opportunity, the time, or the resources necessary to dig deeply into the study of metaphysics up to this point are the target audience for this course. It is geared toward those who want results and are ready to use the conclusions of science as a basis for action without delving into the myriad of processes via which those conclusions were arrived at. Those who want results and are ready to use the conclusions of science as a basis for action will find this to be useful.

It is my expectation that the reader would take the assertions that I make on faith in the same manner that he would take declarations concerning a rule of electrical action if they were published by Marconi or Edison. Accepting these claims at face value, he will demonstrate the truth of them by acting in line with them without displaying any evidence of fear or reluctance in order to prove that they are true. If one accomplishes this, one will surely get wealthy. This is true for both male and female individuals.

The science that is detailed in this book is an exact science, and there is no room for error under any circumstances. But, in order for persons who are interested in researching philosophical theories and developing a rational basis for their opinions to gain something from what I have to say, I will cite a few authors.

Hindu philosophy is the origin of the monistic theory of the universe, which asserts that there is only one substance that appears to manifest itself as the numerous components of the material world. This school of thought has been slowly making its way into the way people think in Western nations over the course of the past two hundred years.

It is the foundation upon which all Eastern philosophies are built and may be found in the writings of Western intellectuals such as Descartes, Spinoza, Leibnitz, Schopenhauer, and Emerson, amongst others. If the reader chooses to study the philosophical background, it is suggested that he or she read Hegel and Emerson themselves.

I wanted my book to be accessible to as many people as possible, so I purposely wrote it in an easy-to-understand style. The following course of action has been tried and tested extensively, and it satisfies the most fundamental condition for any practical experiment: that it be successful. If you are interested in learning how the results were arrived at, I recommend that you read the writings of the authors whose names I gave above.

If you want to see the effects of putting their ideas into practice, you need to read this book and be sure to carry out each of the directions exactly as they are stated in order to see those outcomes.

The ageless song "Money, money, money – must be funny, it is a rich man's world" by Abba may have topped the charts thirty years ago, but the message that it portrays is just as vital now as it was then. The song was written by Björn Ulvaeus and Agnetha Faltskog. In the year 2023, both men and women are enjoying unprecedented levels of wealth, and this success in our financial life provides us with a sense of comfort, security, and satisfaction in our lives.

Despite the fact that some people have been blessed with the ability to inherit wealth or win the lottery, a considerably bigger number of people have built successful businesses by accepting risks that they have carefully considered.

The Institute of Directors is thrilled to be able to offer its assistance and motivation to these individuals who have begun their own enterprises.

The global economy has taken a hit as a result of the collapse of the housing market in the United States and the associated crisis in the subprime mortgage industry. As a result, fifty out of fifty-two stock markets have experienced a loss in value over the course of the past year.

As a result of weaker growth and ongoing inflation, the United Kingdom's economy is on the verge of entering the phase that is the most uncertain it has been in the past 15 years, and there is a possibility that it may plunge into recession.

As a result of this, it will be significantly more challenging to amass wealth, safeguard it, and hand it along to subsequent generations.

This book's objective is to provide the reader with an understanding of the many investment opportunities that are open to them so that they may make informed decisions that are tailored to their specific objectives and level of comfort with risk.

It covers a broad range of topics, such as estate preparation, tax planning, security, and insurance, in addition to providing financial advice that ranges from residential property to pensions, hedge funds, and hobby investments like art and antiques.

In addition to that, it provides services in estate planning. Understanding the relationship between the potential risk of an investment and the potential reward is crucial in order to establish a methodical strategy for wealth management and finally achieve success. The goal of this understanding is to ultimately achieve success.

This book was produced by recognized specialists and is, therefore, a significant resource for high-net-worth individuals as well as those who desire to become high-net-worth individuals since it offers plain and practical guidance without the use of legal jargon.

Reading it could turn out to be the best investment one ever makes in increasing their capacity to handle their financial situation and make sound decisions.

UNDERSTAND YOUR CURRENT FINANCIAL SITUATION

Managing money is an essential part of adult life, yet many people struggle with it. Whether it's living paycheck to paycheck, not having enough savings, or struggling with debt, the first step to improving your financial situation is to take stock of your current situation.

You need to know where your money is going before you can start managing it better.

The most basic step to understanding your current financial situation is to record all your regular monthly income and expenses. This means taking stock of all the money coming in each month, including your paycheck, any rental income, or other sources of income. Then, you need to take stock of all your expenses, including rent, utilities, groceries, entertainment, and any other regular payments.

If you're not used to tracking your finances, this may seem overwhelming at first. However, there are many apps available that can automate the process, making it easier to categorize spending. Some popular options include Mint, PocketGuard, and Simplify by Quicken.

These apps can sync to your financial accounts, automatically categorize spending, and provide you with reports that show you where your money is going.

If you're not comfortable linking your bank account to an app, another option is to save receipts for a month to determine where your money is spent beyond major bills like rent, utilities, and debt payments. This approach can be more time-consuming, but it can also be a wake-up call to realize how much is being spent on items such as groceries or dining out.

It's also important to take stock of any debt you may have. This includes credit card debt, student loans, and any other outstanding loans. Make a list of each debt, the interest rate, and the monthly payment. This will help you understand how much debt you have and how long it will take to pay it off.

Working with a professional is another way to understand your current financial situation, and it may be possible to find this help for free. Many banks and credit unions offer free financial health checkups in their branches. These sessions can provide valuable insights into your current financial situation and help you develop a plan to improve it.

When you're taking stock of your current financial situation, it's important to be honest with yourself. Don't try to hide expenses or downplay the amount of debt you have. Only by being honest with yourself can you develop a realistic plan to improve your financial situation.

Once you have a clear understanding of your current financial situation, you can start to develop a plan to manage your money better. This plan should take into account your current income, expenses, and debt. It should also set realistic goals for saving and paying off debt.

One of the best ways to manage your money better is to create a budget. This involves setting limits on your spending in different categories, such as groceries, entertainment, and dining out. A budget can help you prioritize your spending and make sure you're living within your means.

It's also important to start building an emergency fund. This is a fund of money that you set aside for unexpected expenses, such as car repairs, medical bills, or a job loss.

The amount you need to save depends on your individual circumstances, but most experts recommend saving at least three to six months' worth of expenses.

Another important step to managing your money better is to start paying off debt. This can be a daunting task, but it's essential if you want to improve your financial situation. Start by paying off the debt with the highest interest rate first, as this will save you the most money in the long run.

In addition to paying off debt, it's also important to start saving for the future. This can include saving for retirement, a down payment on a home, or other long-term goals.

Even small amounts of savings can add up over time, so it's important to make saving a habit. One way to do this is to set up automatic transfers from your checking account to a savings account each month.

This way, you won't even have to think about saving - it will happen automatically. Another way to make saving a habit is to track your progress and celebrate your successes along the way. This can help you stay motivated and focused on your long-term financial goals.

By taking stock of your current financial situation and developing a plan to manage your money better, you can take control of your finances and work towards a more secure financial future.

SET PERSONAL PRIORITIES AND FINANCE GOALS

When it comes to managing your finances, it is vital to examine your values and priorities in order to develop a budget that is actually aligned with your objectives. This can be done by thinking about how you want to spend your money and what is most important to you. Understanding what aspects of your life are most important to you and how your financial resources might assist you in achieving those goals is more important than just calculating your income and spending.

According to Ron Oden, an authority on personal finance, "You don't have one goal in life. You have multiple goals." When it comes to creating objectives for your finances, having this frame of mind is essential, as it enables you to take a more comprehensive approach to managing your money. Consider all of the numerous objectives you have and how your money may support them rather than concentrating all of your attention on a single objective, such as paying off debt or preparing for retirement.

Taking a deeper look at your present financial position is one method to evaluate the values and priorities that are most important to you. This may involve a review of your income, costs, and debt, as well as an examination of your spending patterns and the determination of areas in which you might make reductions in spending. You may start to make decisions that are more thoughtful with regard to your finances after you have a better grasp of where your money is going and what you are presently prioritizing.

For instance, if spending quality time with your family is one of your highest priorities, you may want to think about hiring a cleaning service or other similar service in order to free up more of your time so that you can devote it to spending time with your family. On the other hand, if going on vacation is a higher priority for you than other kinds of spending, you may want to save more money for future trips and spend less on other kinds of costs that are not as essential to you.

When it comes to establishing your financial priorities, it is essential to broaden your focus beyond the immediate future and take into account not only long-term but also intermediate objectives. These may vary from putting money aside for a relatively little purchase, such as a new piece of furniture or a nice night out, to putting money toward a more extravagant purchase, such as a luxury trip or an investment in a long-term retirement plan.

Finding a balance between the things that are important to you in the near term and the things that will matter to you in the long run is the key to success. Since you will be saving money for things that really matter to you and that thrill you, this may be an effective strategy for maintaining your financial motivation and staying on track with your financial goals.

To really bring your principles into alignment with your financial decisions, you should avoid putting unnecessary restrictions on yourself. Do not be afraid to dream large and create objectives that are challenging for yourself, even if they seem unattainable at the moment. You will be able to make progress over time and finally realize your greater vision if you first break down these more substantial objectives into smaller, more doable tasks.

In addition to this, it is essential to examine your financial strategy on a monthly basis and make any adjustments. Because of the unpredictable nature of life, your priorities may vary as time goes on. You can make sure that you are staying on track with your financial objectives by checking in with yourself on a frequent basis and reevaluating them. This will also allow you to change your budget appropriately as necessary.

It is necessary to have a firm grasp of fundamental financial concepts such as budgeting, saving, and investing, in addition to having financial objectives that have been defined for one's financial situation. This may include keeping a record of your expenditures, developing a financial plan, and looking for opportunities to save costs on routine purchases. If you have a solid foundation in these areas, you will be better able to make informed choices about your finances that are in line with your beliefs and the objectives you want to achieve.

When it comes to obtaining financial stability and success, one of the most important factors is making sure that your personal finances are in line with your core principles. You will be able to feel more confident in your financial future and make decisions that are more thoughtful with your money if you take the time to discover what matters most to you and then develop objectives that reflect those values. This will give you more control over your financial destiny. Whether you are trying to put money down for a new house, prepare for retirement, or just want to live a life that is more rewarding overall, basing your financial decisions on your core beliefs will help you move closer to achieving your goals.

CREATE AND STICK TO A BUDGET

Everyone needs to get into the habit of creating and sticking to a budget since it is one of the most fundamental financial practices. It may not be difficult to design a budget that outlines how your monthly money will be spent, but sticking to the budget is often a difficulty for most people. Individuals may not have the self-control to limit impulsive purchases, or they may feel too constrained when forced to plan their spending in advance. Another possibility is that people may not want to plan their spending in advance. Yet, if you are able to stay within your budget, you will be rewarded with extra income that you can spend on the things that are most important to you.

Finding out how much money you bring in is the first thing you need to do when making a budget. This covers salary, bonuses, and any and all other streams of revenue, as well as any and all other sources of income. When you have calculated your revenue, the next step is to arrange your costs in descending order of importance. You should prioritize spending your money on items like your mortgage or rent payment, your utilities, and your groceries. Following that, you will be able to distribute cash to cover your other costs.

It is essential to have a distinct comprehension of your monetary objectives before beginning the process of budgeting for your household. These objectives can include getting rid of existing debt, putting money down for a down payment on a house, or establishing an emergency savings account. If you have a crystal clear grasp of your financial objectives, it will be much easier for you to make sound choices about your finances and maintain the motivation necessary to stick to your budget.

While putting out a budget, it is essential to be as practical as possible. It will be difficult for you to stick to your spending plan if you establish expectations for yourself that are not realistic. You should always be sure to budget for unforeseen costs, such as those associated with medical treatment or automobile maintenance. Being truthful with yourself about the ways in which you spend money is another essential step. If you are aware that you have a propensity for buying online, you should include some cash in your financial plan to accommodate this weakness.

After you have finally finished making your budget, the true battle will begin: sticking to it. It is simple to put out a spending plan, but it requires self-control to really keep to it. Reminding yourself of the financial objectives you have set for yourself is one strategy for maintaining your motivation. Remind yourself of your objectives and how the item you want to buy will have an effect on those objectives whenever you have the impulse to make an impulsive purchase.

Rewarding yourself for adhering to your financial plan is another technique to keep yourself motivated. This might be something as easy as taking yourself out to a good meal or seeing a movie as a reward.

If you realize that there is not enough money to pay for all that you would want, look for methods to reduce your spending in order to make up the difference. When it comes to cutting costs, one common piece of advice is to get rid of tiny, recurrent payments like redundant streaming services or takeaway coffee. Nevertheless, it is important not to overlook bigger, more sporadic expenditures. It is possible that you are unaware of how simple it might be to cut costs that are conventionally seen as being fixed. You may, for instance, refinance your home to bring down your monthly payment or negotiate a better deal on your auto insurance. Both of these options could help you save money.

You may decrease costs in other areas of your life by looking for methods to minimize the amount you spend on things like your utilities. You might reduce your energy use by installing a programmed thermostat, switching to energy-efficient light bulbs, or using a power strip to turn off gadgets when they are not being used. The cumulative effect of these inconspicuous adjustments might lead to cost savings on your regular expenses over time.

In addition to this, you should pay close attention to the ways in which you spend money. If you discover that you are spending too much money in a certain area, you should seek methods to reduce your expenditure in that area. You may, for instance, begin meal planning or shop in bulk in order to save money if you find that you are spending an excessive amount on groceries. You might seek things to do with your friends and family that are either completely free or not very expensive if you find that you are spending too much money on entertainment.

In conclusion, creating a budget that outlines how your monthly revenue will be spent may be a simple and straightforward process. But adhering to it is sometimes a difficult task. Individuals may not have the self-control to limit impulsive purchases, or they may feel too constrained when forced to plan their spending in advance. Another possibility is that people may not want to plan their spending in advance. Yet, if you are able to stay within your budget, you will be rewarded with extra income that you can spend on the things that are most important to you. In addition to this, it will be much simpler to stick to a budget if it is created with your objectives and goals in mind when it is being created. You may effectively keep to your budget and reach your financial objectives if you are realistic, observant of the ways in which you spend money, and proactive in minimizing the amount of money you spend. Keep in mind that a budget is a tool that may assist you in regaining control of your money and in improving the overall quality of your life. It is possible that initially, it may be difficult, but the rewards will make it worthwhile. You may develop a habit of budgeting if you are disciplined and persistent, and then you can reap the benefits of having financial stability and security.

THE RIGHT TO BE RICH

No matter how much praise one might heap upon living in abject destitution, the undeniable truth is that in order to have a life that is really full and successful, one has to be wealthy. If a person does not have a sufficient amount of money, they will never be able to develop their talents or their souls to their full potential.

It is impossible for him to develop his ability or his soul if he does not have access to a wide variety of tools, and he cannot have these tools unless he has the financial means to purchase them.

Humans grow intellectually, spiritually, and physically by interaction with the material world, and because of the way society is structured, individuals need money in order to acquire the means to participate in that world. Thus, the science of affluence ought to serve as the foundation for all future developments in human civilization.

The progression of one's life is the purpose of living in general. Anything that has the potential to live should have the unalienable right to all of the growth it is capable of achieving.

The right to life of a person includes the right to have the free and unrestricted use of all the goods that may be essential to the complete mental, spiritual, and physical blossoming of that person; in other words, the right to be wealthy.

In this book, I will not be referring to wealth in a figurative sense in any manner. Being really wealthy does not imply being happy or satisfied with having just a little amount of anything. Nobody needs to be content with a little amount if they are able to use and enjoy a greater quantity of anything else. The progression and improvement of life are what the natural world is working toward. Every single person ought to have access to everything that might enhance the power, elegance, beauty, and richness of their existence.

A wealthy person is one who has all that he needs or desires in order to live the fullest life that he is capable of living. Without a significant amount of money, no one can have all they want. Because of how far life has progressed and how complicated it has gotten, even the most commonplace man or woman needs a significant amount of cash in order to live in a way that even comes close to being comprehensive. This drive to actualize one's latent potential is an essential part of the human condition and is present in every individual by virtue of the fact that people are naturally inclined to pursue their full potential. Being who you see yourself to be is the key to achieving success in life. You can only become what you want to be by making use of things, and you can only have the free use of things if you have achieved a level of financial success that allows you to purchase them. Because of this, having a solid grasp of the economics behind amassing wealth is the single most important skill you can have.

There is nothing wrong with having the goal of being wealthy. The desire for wealth is, at its core, the desire for a life that is fuller, more satisfying, and more plentiful. This aspiration is certainly deserving of admiration. Rare is the individual who does not have the aspiration to live a life of greater plenty. And the person who does not wish to have enough money to acquire whatever he wants could not be living up to his full potential as a human being.

We live for three different reasons: the body, the mind, and the spirit. These are the three things that keep us going. There is no one of them that is superior to the others or more holy. Each one is desired, but neither the body, the intellect, nor the spirit can live to its fullest potential if one of the others is deprived of the opportunity to completely live and express themselves. To spend one's life in such a way as to prioritize one's spirit above one's intellect or body is neither right nor honorable. It is unethical to base one's existence on one's intellect while denying one's body and soul.

Living for one's physical form while ignoring one's mental and spiritual selves always results in repugnant consequences, as we are all well aware of. It is clear to us that living a true life implies giving one's fullest expression of everything that they are capable of giving via their body, mind, and spirit. There is no way for a person to be really content or happy until all aspects of their being, including their mind, body, and soul, are functioning to their maximum potential. Only then can they experience genuine joy and satisfaction. Unfulfilled desires may be found everywhere. There is a potential that is not being fully realized or a role that is not being fully carried out. A desire is a potential or a function that is looking for an expression of itself or a performance.

A person's physical life cannot be lived to its fullest potential if they do not have access to healthy food, suitable clothes, a safe and warm place to live, and freedom from excessive manual labor. A healthy balance between work and play is essential to his physical well-being.

It is impossible for him to completely exist in his mind if he does not have access to books and the time to study them, if he does not have the chance to travel and observe, and if he does not have intellectual companionship. In order for him to experience life to the fullest, he has to engage in intellectual pursuits and surround himself with as many works of art and beautiful things as he is capable of using and enjoying.

One needs to have love in their life in order to truly exist in their spirit. Yet the expression of love is often thwarted by financial constraints.

Giving to the people you care about most gives a person the deepest sense of fulfillment and satisfaction. Giving is the activity in which love most clearly manifests itself in a natural and unforced way. A person who has nothing to offer cannot adequately fulfill the roles of husband or father, citizen or human being since they have nothing to provide. A person finds full life for his body, develops his intellect, and unfolds his soul via the use of material objects. This is how a person finds full life. Because of this, having a lot of money is really important. It is very appropriate for you to have the goal of attaining great wealth. It is impossible to avoid doing so if you are a normal person, whether you are male or female. Since it is both the most honorable and the most important of all fields of study, the science of becoming wealthy is deserving of your undivided focus. It is completely appropriate for you to do so. If you fail to make time for this study, you will be shirking your responsibility to yourself, God, and the rest of mankind. There is no greater duty you can provide for God or for mankind than to become the best version of yourself.

THERE IS A SCIENCE OF GETTING RICH

There is a methodical approach to achieving financial success. It is a precise science comparable to algebra or mathematics in its approach. The path to financial success is governed by a set of rules that must be followed in order to achieve success. When a person understands and abides by these principles, it is mathematically assured that they will amass great wealth.

Following a certain course of action will lead to the accumulation of wealth, both monetary and physical in kind. Individuals that conduct themselves in this particular manner, whether by intention or by chance, find themselves in a position of financial success. People who do not conduct themselves in this particular manner will, regardless of how hard they work or how much ability they possess, continue to live in poverty.

According to the rule of nature, results that are consistent with their causes are always produced. Thus, any man or woman who learns to do things in this particular manner will always become wealthy. This applies to both men and women. The following evidence demonstrates that the aforementioned assertion is accurate.

It is not dependent on one's surroundings to get wealthy. If that were the case, everyone living in particular regions would suddenly find themselves flush with cash. Those living in one city would have a high standard of living, while others in other places would live in abject poverty. The people living in one state would be living lavishly, whilst others in the state next door would be struggling to make ends meet.

Rich and poor people may be seen coexisting in the same communities and usually working in the same occupations rather regularly. When two persons live in the same community and work in the same line of work, but one of them becomes wealthy while the other continues to live in poverty, this demonstrates that being wealthy is not largely a matter of environment. It is possible that some environments are more favorable than others; however, when two people in the same business are in the same neighborhood, and one succeeds in becoming wealthy while the other does not, this demonstrates that becoming wealthy is the result of doing things in a particular manner.

And also, the capacity to accomplish things in this particular manner is not entirely attributable to the existence of skill, as shown by the fact that many individuals who have a great deal of talent nonetheless live in poverty, and others who have very little talent become extremely wealthy.

When we research the characteristics of wealthy individuals, we discover that, on the whole, they are not much different from the general population. It is obvious that the reason they are wealthy is not due to the exceptional qualities and capabilities that they possess. When they happen to do things in a specific manner, they end up with a lot of money.

There is no correlation between frugality and financial success. Those who are very frugal often find themselves in a position of poverty, in contrast to those who have no problem spending freely and often find themselves in a position of wealth.

Neither is becoming wealthy as a result of accomplishing things that other people fail to do. When two persons in the same industry engage in almost identical activities, it is not uncommon for one of them to achieve financial success while the other struggles to make ends meet or even declares bankruptcy.

Because of all of these factors, we have no choice but to draw the conclusion that being wealthy is the consequence of conducting one's life in a certain manner.

If being rich is the outcome of doing things in a certain manner, then everyone who is capable of doing things in that way has the potential to become wealthy. This applies to both men and women. And if the same causes always yield identical results, then the whole topic may be brought within the purview of a precise scientific discipline.

The issue that has to be asked is whether or not this particular path is so challenging that very few people will be able to take it. As we have shown, this cannot be true with regard to a person's innate talent. Riches come to those with talent but also to those with stupid ideas. Riches may be attained by those with high levels of intellectual capacity as well as by those with low levels of intelligence. Those who are physically strong tend to amass wealth, as do those who are physically weak or ill.

It goes without saying that a certain level of mental capacity and comprehension is required. If a person, regardless of gender, has the mental capacity to read and comprehend the information presented here, then that person has a natural skill that makes it possible for them to become wealthy.

Even if we have shown that it is not a question of the environment, it is still important to note that location is important for anything. It is unrealistic to think that one could do effective business in the middle of the Sahara Desert.

Dealing with other people and being in environments where there are other people to deal with are both required if one wants to become wealthy. Nonetheless, it is roughly the extent to which the environment is relevant. If others in your community are successful in accumulating wealth, then too can you. You have just as much of a chance of becoming wealthy as everyone else in your state.

To reiterate, it is not a question of selecting a certain industry or line of work to pursue. Persons are able to become wealthy in every industry and in every profession, even when their next-door neighbors who work the same job continue to live in abject poverty.

It is a well-known fact that if you work in a field that interests you, you will be more successful. In addition, if you have certain abilities that you have honed through time, you will find the most success in a line of work that allows you to put those talents to good use.

You will have the most success if you choose a line of work that is appropriate for the region in which you live. If you wanted to open an ice cream shop, the best location would be somewhere warmer than Greenland. It is more likely that a salmon fishery will be successful in the Pacific Northwest than it is in the state of Florida, which does not have salmon.

Apart from these more fundamental constraints, however, being wealthy is not contingent on your working in a particular industry; rather, it is based on your learning to carry out activities in a certain fashion. If you are now in business but are not becoming money despite being in the same line of work as someone else in your community, the reason for this is likely due to the fact that you are not doing things in the same manner that the other person is approaching them.

Lack of funds is never an obstacle on the path to financial success for anybody. It is correct that as your money grows, its expansion will become less difficult and quicker. Yet, regardless of how low your current financial situation may be, if you start acting in a certain manner, you will start amassing cash. Acquiring financial resources is a necessary step on the path to financial success and plenty. It is an aspect of the end outcome that always comes about as a direct consequence of acting in a certain manner.

Even if you are the poorest person on the continent and have a lot of debt, if you start doing things in this particular manner, you will always start to become wealthy. You will get wealthy regardless of whether or not you have any friends, influence, or other resources since similar causes always yield similar consequences. If you have no capital, you can obtain capital. If you are now in the incorrect line of work, you may transition into the line of work that better suits you. In the event that you are at the incorrect place, you have the option of moving to the correct spot. You are able to accomplish this goal by commencing in your existing company and in your current location to conduct activities in a certain manner that leads to success.

CAN OPPORTUNITIES BE CONTROLLED?

Nobody lives in abject poverty because other people have hoarded all of the riches and built a wall around it, thereby denying other people access to the opportunities that would otherwise be available to them.

Instead, nobody lives in abject poverty because nobody has built a wall around the riches. You have the choice to abstain from engaging in some kinds of commercial activity, but in addition to that, you also have access to a variety of alternative possibilities. There is a significant probability that you would have a hard time getting control of any of the big fuel and power-generating firms.

There is a good likelihood that this would be the case. Companies that use alternative forms of energy, such as solar energy and electricity generated by wind and other natural forces, are still in their infancy and have a tremendous amount of potential for growth; companies that use traditional forms of energy, such as fossil fuels, are well established and have little room for expansion. Solar energy is an example of one of these types of businesses.

It will only be a matter of a few years until new technologies of communication and transportation (such as electric autos, space travel, microwave transmission, etc.) become accessible in forms that are radically different from what is now envisioned for them. These will develop into major industries that will be able to provide work opportunities to tens of thousands, hundreds of thousands, and even millions of people. Why do not you concentrate on building these firms instead of attempting to compete with the huge corporations for possibilities in the business world? This would be a far more productive use of your time.

If you are a worker who is employed by a power-producing plant, the likelihood of you ever becoming the owner of the facility in which you work is very low due to the nature of your employment. This is something that is completely accurate in every way. On the other hand, it is also a fact that if you start behaving in a particular manner, you will soon be in a position to quit your job at the power company, buy a farm that is between ten and forty acres in size, and start working there as a producer of natural foodstuffs and organic products.

If you act in this manner, you will be able to do so. You may accomplish this goal by starting to behave in a certain manner. You may also try your hand at hydroponic farming, which differs from traditional gardening in that it involves growing plants in nutrient solutions rather than soil and provides substantial crops despite the little area required.

There has recently been a considerable increase in the number of opportunities available on the market for both men and women to participate in the organic agriculture of small plots of land. You may say that it is impossible for you to get the land, but I am going to prove to you that it is not impossible; that you can certainly get a farm if you are willing to go to work in a certain way. If you say that it is impossible for you to get the land, I am going to prove to you that it is not impossible. You could think that it is impossible for you to get the land, but I am going to show you that it is not impossible by proving to you that it is doable.

The tide of opportunity moves in different directions at different periods, according to the needs of the whole and to the particular degree of social development that has been attained. This is because the requirements of the whole change over time. This is the situation due to the fact that the requirements are placed on the entire shift throughout time. At this time in the United States of America, there is a tendency toward decentralization, as well as a trend toward industries that can be decentralized. In addition, there is a trend toward industries that can be decentralized.

In today's environment, farmers that practice sustainable agriculture by relying on organic and herbal methods have access to more options than office employees do. An executive who spends their days running on the corporate treadmill has fewer opportunities available to them than a businessman who works in the area of environmentally friendly and alternative types of energy because the former spends their days running on the treadmill and the latter works in the field.

If a person is ready to go with the flow of things rather than trying to swim against it, they will discover that there are many more options open to them.

There is a wealth of opportunity available to office workers, both on an individual level and in the context of the workforce as a whole. Workers, who are the true rulers of major businesses and conglomerates, are not being repressed by the power that these institutions wield. Because of the method in which they carry out their activities, they have arrived at this stage as a group owing to the fact that they have progressed to this degree.

The working class has the capacity to become the master class if it adopts a specific way of conducting its activities. This potential can only be realized, however, if the working class takes action. According to the law of wealth, it operates in accordance with the same set of guidelines as all of the other groupings. As long as workers maintain the same level of productivity that they have traditionally enjoyed, there will be no change in the location of their place of employment. The individual worker, on the other hand, is not held back by the intellectual sloth or ignorance of his class; rather, he has the ability to ride the wave of opportunity all the way to financial success. This is in contrast to the collective worker class, which is held back by both of these factors. This book will instruct him on how to do it.

Someone in a continued state of poverty is not always caused by a limited supply of riches in their environment. There is more than enough for everyone to get their fill without worrying about running out. The amount of construction material that is available in the United States by itself is sufficient to build a palace for every household on the planet that is as large as the capital building in Washington. This is because the United States has access to such a large quantity of construction material. If this country were to apply more intensive agricultural techniques, it would have the ability to produce enough wool, cotton, linen, silk, and food to clothe and feed every person in the world. It would seem that there is an almost infinite supply of things that may be seen. In addition, the hidden supply really does have an infinite amount of resources available to it.

Everything that you see on earth starts from a single fundamental component, which acts as the seed from which all other things develop. This fundamental component is known as the "primordial soup." There is a continual development of new forms, while at the same time, older forms are dissolved; yet, these new forms are only various expressions of the same thing.

Either the supply of formless material or the supply of original substance is endless and cannot be depleted to any point. In spite of the fact that it makes up the whole of the universe, not all of it was consumed in the creation of the cosmos. The original substance, which is formless matter and the raw material from which all things are constructed, may be found permeating and filling the spaces in, through, and between the forms that make up the visible universe. These spaces are then filled with the original material after being penetrated by it. The supply of universal raw material will not be exhausted even if another ten thousand universes are produced since there is still plenty of it. This is because there is still enough of it.

Due to this, no one can be said to be destitute on the basis that nature is lacking or that there is not enough to go around. This is because there is always more than enough for everyone.

There is an almost unfathomable amount of richness that may be discovered in nature. This resource will never be in low supply under any circumstances. The original essence is always giving birth to new forms since it is throbbing with the creative power of the cosmos and is perpetually expanding. After the current supply of building materials has been depleted, further materials will be created to fill the void left by the previous batch. After the soil has been utilized to its maximum capacity, meaning that plants that supply food and fiber for clothing cannot grow on it any longer, either the earth will be repaired or more soil will be generated. As soon as all of the gold and silver that can be extracted from the earth has been done so, more will be formed from the formless. This is based on the assumption that individuals made by humans are still at a stage of social development where they have a desire for gold and silver. The formless material is sensitive to the needs of people; it will not let them be deprived of any aspect that might be beneficial to them in any way.

This is something that can be said about the whole of humankind. The average wealth of each individual member of the race is very high. People are impoverished because they do not adhere to a certain way of carrying out activities that result in financial success for the person undertaking those activities on his own.

The formless element has intelligence; it is the substance itself that is thinking. It is alive, and as a result, it is constantly striving to produce new life for itself and for others.

Being a living entity brings with it the desire to enjoy one's life to the fullest, and this desire is totally acceptable. It is typical of intellect to strive toward increasing its scope, and it is characteristic of awareness to work toward expanding its area of effect and reaching a greater depth of expression. Both of these characteristics are inborn. Formless living creatures flung themselves into form in order to express themselves more thoroughly and, as a result, establish the universe of forms. This formless living entity is responsible for the production of the world of forms.

The universe is a massive living presence that is continually and inexorably advancing toward greater life and a higher degree of functioning. Its development cannot be stopped or reversed.

The continuation of life is the fundamental aim of nature and the driving force behind its development; this is its primary purpose. As a consequence of this, everything that may possibly be advantageous to live things is abundantly offered. There is no way that anything could be lacking unless God were to contradict himself and make his own creations pointless in the process of making them. You do not continue to live in poverty just because there is a deficiency in the amount of wealth that is available. I shall demonstrate to you a little bit later on that even the assets of the formless supply are controllable by any man or woman who is ready to act and think in a certain way.

46

THE LAW OF THOUGHTS

The only force capable of generating material wealth from a formless substance is the human mind's capacity for thought. One thinkable substance serves as the raw material for the creation of all other things. The formation of form in this material is triggered by the concept of form.

The original material will behave in a certain way based on its thinking. Every structure and action that you can see in the natural world is the outward manifestation of a notion that was there in the primary material. When it considers a shape, it immediately assumes that form; when it considers a motion, it immediately enacts that motion. It is the process through which everything comes into being. Our home is a thought world, and our thought world is a component of a larger thought universe.

The idea of a changing world permeated the whole formless material and spread outward from there. The thinking material that emerged as a consequence of that thought adopted the shape of planetary systems and has successfully preserved that appearance to this day. The idea of a thinking material causes it to take on the shape of the thought, and it also causes it to move in accordance with the concept. It had the concept of a revolving system of suns and planets in its head, so it assumed the shape of these bodies and moved them in the appropriate manner.

Even if it may take millennia to complete the task, all that is necessary is to visualize the shape of a slow-growing tree in order for the formless material to construct the tree. Throughout the process of creation, the formless material seems to move along the lines of motion that it has already constructed. The mere idea of an oak tree does not immediately generate a fully developed tree, but it does set in action the forces that will eventually construct the tree following predetermined lines of development.

Every idea of form, when retained in thinking matter, causes the production of that form; nevertheless, every thought of form produces the development of that form always, or at least typically, following lines of growth and activity that have previously been established.

Even if an impression of a home with a particular layout were made onto the formless material, it is possible that this would not immediately result in the production of that structure. Yet, as a consequence of this, creative forces that are currently at work in business and commerce would be redirected into other channels, which would lead to the accelerated construction of the home. And if there were no pre-existing pathways through which the creative force might operate, the home would be constructed straight from the elemental material, bypassing the time-consuming processes that are inherent in the organic and inorganic worlds.

There is no way to impose an idea of the shape onto the primary material without inducing the production of that form.

A human person is both a center for thought and a source of thought in their own right. It is necessary for a person's thoughts to give birth to all of the shapes that he or she creates with their hands. Before he can give anything physical form, he must first think about it.

And up until this point, man has focused all of his efforts on the job that he does with his hands; he has applied physical labor to the world of forms in an attempt to alter or improve forms that already exist. He has not given any attention to the possibility of attempting to imprint his ideas on the formless material in order to bring about the formation of new forms.

When a person has a thought form, he creates a picture of the shape that is in his head by taking material from the forms found in nature and combining it with his own imagination. At this point, he has not made much of an effort, if any at all, to collaborate with the formless intelligence in order to work "with the Father." He has never even entertained the notion that he is capable of "do what he seeth the Father doing." With physical effort, man is able to change and alter preexisting forms. He has not given any attention to the topic of whether or not he is capable of creating objects out of formless material by transmitting his ideas to it. It is my intention to demonstrate not just that he is capable of doing so but also that any person, regardless of gender, is capable of doing so and of demonstrating how. My initial move will be to state three premises that are crucial to the discussion.

To begin, we are going to make the assumption that there is one primordial, formless material that all things are constructed. Every one of the seemingly many components is, in reality, only several presentations of the same element. The myriad distinct forms that may be seen in biological and inorganic nature are all just various configurations of the same material. Furthermore, this substance is thinking stuff; when thought is kept in it, the form of the concept is produced. The formation of forms results from the operation of thought on thinking material. An individual has the capacity for unique and creative cognition thanks to their brain. If a person is able to convey the content of their thought to the original thinking material, they will be able to bring about the production or formation of the item that they are thinking about. In a nutshell, this means:

There is a thinking stuff from which all things are produced and which, in its natural condition, pervades, penetrates, and fills the interspaces of the world. All things are made of this thinking stuff.

The manifestation of the object that is envisioned by thought in this material is caused by a thought.

A person is able to construct things in his thoughts, and then, by impressing those thoughts into formless matter, he may bring about the creation of the things he thinks about.

Both logic and personal experience support my ability to establish these assertions. After working my way backward through the phenomena of form and mind, I have arrived at the conclusion that there is one original thinking material. Continuing my line of thought from the thinking substance, I arrive at the conclusion that a person has the ability to bring about the materialization of the item that occupies his or her thoughts.

My experience has shown me that this line of reasoning is correct, and this is the most compelling evidence I have. If only one person who reads this book is able to improve his financial situation by following the advice I provide, then that is proof that substantiates my assertion. In addition, unless someone goes through the procedure and is unsuccessful, it cannot be considered conclusive evidence even if everyone follows my instructions and becomes wealthy. The theory is valid up to the point that the process fails, but this process will not fail since everybody who performs precisely what I instruct him to do will end up filthy wealthy.

I have said that one may improve their financial situation by engaging in activities in a certain manner. To be able to accomplish this goal, one needs to train themselves to think in a certain manner. The manner in which a person conducts himself is a direct reflection of the way in which he thinks about many aspects of life.

You will need to have the capacity to think in the way that you want to think in order to accomplish things in the manner in which you want to do them. This is the first step on the path to financial success. Regardless of how things may look, the only way to get to the truth is to think about what you want to believe.

Every individual has the natural and innate capacity to think whatever it is that they want to think; nevertheless, it takes a great deal more work to do so than it does to think the ideas that are suggested by appearances. To think in accordance with one's look is a simple task. To consider truth regardless of appearances is arduous and needs the expenditure of more power than any other activity that an individual is required to undertake.

There is no kind of labor from which the majority of people shy away as much as they do from that of continuous and consecutive contemplation; it is the most difficult form of labor in the universe. This is particularly true in situations when the truth runs counter to first impressions. Every occurrence in the world that can be seen has the propensity to generate a comparable shape in the mind of the one who witnesses it. Keeping the notion of the truth in one's mind is the sole defense against this possibility.

Just contemplating the outward manifestations of sickness might cause that person to manifest those symptoms in their own thoughts and, eventually, their own body. Instead, you need to have the concept that there is no sickness in your head at all times. This is the reality. The only thing that really exists is health; disease is only an appearance.

Just seeing the outward manifestations of poverty will cause comparable thoughts to emerge in your own head. You should instead insist on the reality that there is no such thing as poverty. There is simply a plentiful supply.

To think of one's health while the outward signs of sickness surround one or to think of one's wealth when one is surrounded by the outward signs of poverty takes a great deal of mental strength. Yet whoever has this power transforms into a master thinker capable of overcoming destiny and achieving everything he sets his mind to.

This power can only be obtained by grasping the fundamental truth that lies underlying all appearances, which is that there is one thinking material from which and by which all things are formed. Acquiring this knowledge is the only way to achieve this power.

Next, we have to come to terms with the fact that every idea that is kept in this material takes the shape of a form and that a person may exert his thoughts on this substance in order to cause those thoughts to take shape and become objects that can be seen.

When we have this understanding, we are freed from any doubt and worry because we are confident in our ability to bring into existence whatever it is that our hearts want. Both the things we want to acquire and the people we want to become are within our reach. If you want to become wealthy, the first thing you need to do is believe the three essential assertions that were presented earlier on in this chapter. In order to stress them more, I will state them once again here:

There is a thinking stuff from which all things are produced and which, in its unaltered state, pervades, penetrates, and fills the interspaces of the world. All things are made of this thinking stuff.

The manifestation of the object that is envisioned by thought in this material is caused by a thought.

A person is able to construct things in his thoughts, and then, by impressing those thoughts into formless matter, he may bring about the creation of the things he thinks about.

You are required to give up any and all other ideas about the universe in favor of this monistic one. You need to give something a lot of consideration in order for it to become ingrained in your consciousness and a regular part of your mental process. Repeatedly reading these tenets will help you internalize their meaning. Commit every phrase to memory and reflect on them until you can affirm with absolute certainty that they mean what they say. In the event that you are troubled by uncertainty, see it as an act of sin and put it out of your mind.

You should not pay attention to anyone who argues against this notion, and you should not attend churches or seminars where people preach or teach a different perspective on things. Avoid reading any books or journals that promote an alternative philosophy. If you let your religious beliefs cloud your judgment, then none of your efforts will amount to anything.

Do not speculate as to how these things may possibly be real, nor should you wonder why these things are true. So go ahead and put your faith in them.

The first step in mastering the art of amassing wealth is to fully embrace and internalize this faith.

INCREASING LIFE

You have to cast aside any lingering remnants of the outdated notion that there is a god whose desire it is that you should be impoverished or whose objectives may be served by putting you in a state of economic deprivation.

You are home to the conscious entity that permeates the whole universe and can be found residing in every other object. It is a living material that is aware of its own existence. Since it is a deliberately alive material, it must have the natural and innate desire that is present in all living intellect, which is the desire to see more life come into being. Since the sheer act of existing requires it, every living thing has a constant obligation to work toward the extension of its own existence, given that life must grow in order to exist.

When a seed is planted in the earth, it immediately begins to grow, and the process of living results in the production of one hundred additional seeds. Just by existing, life generates more of itself. It never stops growing; this is a necessary condition for its continued existence.

The same pressure to achieve ever-higher levels of intelligence applies to intelligence itself. It is necessary for us to think of another idea after every thought we have since every thought compels us to think of another thought. The scope of consciousness is always being broadened. As we learn one truth, it always leads us to the discovery of another one. The amount of information that is known is continuously growing. The cultivation of one skill always leads to the development of a desire to work on developing more talents. The drive of life exerts its influence on us. In the process of trying to give form to this impulse, we find that we are driven to learn more, to do more, and to be more.

It is only via having more that we may learn more, do more, and become more. It is only via the use of things that we may learn, grow, and develop. Hence it is imperative that we have things at our disposal. We need to get wealthy in order to extend our lives.

The capability for a greater existence that is seeking fulfillment is what drives the desire for wealth; every want is the endeavor of an unrealized possibility to become a reality. The search for manifestation via power is what gives rise to desire. The identical factor that stimulates your desire for more money is also the one that stimulates the plant's growth. It is life itself, searching for a complete manifestation.

During the whole of life, the one living substance must be held accountable to this rule. It is under the requirement of making things because it is saturated with the desire to live more, which is why it is under that obligation. Since this material wants to dwell more fully inside you, it is concerned that you have access to all that you might possibly need.

It is God's will that you be successful in accumulating wealth. He believes that if you have a lot of material possessions, he will have a greater opportunity to express yourself through you. For this reason, he wants you to become wealthy. If you have complete control over the means of survival, he will be able to dwell more fully inside you.

The universe wishes for you to achieve all of your goals and have all you want. Your plans will not be hindered by mother nature. You have no problems with any aspect of life. Convince yourself that what I am saying is correct.

But, it is of the utmost importance that the purpose you want to achieve be congruent with the goal that underlies everything.

You can not settle for simple pleasure or the fulfillment of your senses if you seek true life. Life is the performance of a function, and a person only really lives when he or she performs without excess every function—physical, mental, and spiritual— of which they are capable. Life is defined as the ability to execute these functions.

You do not want to get wealthy so that you may live a swinish lifestyle for the sake of gratifying your primal urges. This is not how life works. But, the execution of each and every bodily function is an essential component of existence, and no one lives their life to its fullest extent if they deny the impulses of their bodies a natural and healthy expression.

You are not interested in amassing wealth for the express purpose of indulging in mental gratification, acquiring knowledge, sating ambition, besting others, or becoming famous. All of these things are legitimate components of life; nevertheless, a person who simply lives for the pleasures of the brain would only have a fragment of a whole existence. He will never be content with the way things have turned out for him.

You are not interested in amassing wealth for the express purpose of improving the lives of other people. You do not want to give up yourself for the sake of saving the world, nor do you want to give up yourself only for the pleasure of helping others and making sacrifices. There is more to life than just reveling in one's inner delights. They are not superior to any other portion in any way, nor are they more honorable.

You want to amass a lot of wealth so that you may enjoy good food and drink and have a good time when the occasion calls for it. You desire to amass wealth so that you may indulge your senses with exquisite objects, broaden your horizons by traveling to far-flung locations, cultivate your mental faculties, and eat well. You want to become wealthy so that you may love other people, be nice to others, and play a positive role in assisting the rest of the world in its search for the truth.

It is important to keep in mind, however, that extreme selflessness is neither more admirable nor better than excessive altruism. Both of these are errors.

Put an end to the notion that God wants you to sacrifice yourself for the sake of other people and that you may win his favor by doing so. God has no such requirements for his followers.

What he really wants is for you to maximize your potential, both for yourself and for the sake of others around you. In addition, the most effective method to assist other people is to develop your own potential to its fullest.

Becoming wealthy is the only way to really maximize your potential as a person. So, it is appropriate and commendable for you to give the process of accumulating riches the foremost and most thoughtful consideration in your life.

Keep in mind, though, that the want for something substantial is universal. Since it is looking for wealth and life in everything and in everyone, its motions need to be for a greater life to be given to everyone, and it cannot be coerced into working to provide less life to anybody.

You will have things made for you with intelligent material, but it will not steal things from other people in order to give them to you.

You have to banish all thoughts of other people from your mind. You are not to compete for what has already been developed but rather to build something new. You are not obligated in any manner to deprive anybody else of anything. It is not necessary for you to drive a hard bargain. You are not required to deceive others or take advantage of them. You are under no obligation to hire any guy at a wage that is lower than the one he already receives.

You are not required to be envious of the possessions of others or to gaze at them with longing in your eyes. There is nothing that someone has that you cannot also get for yourself. And you may have it without robbing him of what he already has in the process.

You ought not to see yourself as a rival but rather as a creator.

You are going to obtain what you desire, but it is going to come to you in such a manner that when you have it, everyone else is going to have more than he has right now.

It has been brought to my attention that there are some who make a significant amount of money by acting in a manner that is diametrically opposed to the instructions given in the previous paragraph. Individuals of the plutocratic kind who amass tremendous wealth often do so only as a result of the exceptional abilities they demonstrate on the battlefield of competition. Yet, there are instances — for instance, when they make a contribution to the expansion of the industry — when they unintentionally accord with the flow of the substance toward the improvement of mankind. Rockefeller, Carnegie, Morgan, and others like them have been the unwitting instruments of the Highest Power in the necessary job of systematizing and organizing productive industry. This labor has been necessary because it was necessary. Their efforts have made a significant contribution toward a higher quality of life for everyone. They contributed to the organization of production but were quickly supplanted by the agents of the mass, who were responsible for organizing the machinery of distribution.

The multimillionaires are comparable to the gigantic animals that roamed the earth during ancient times. They are an essential component of the evolutionary process, but the same force that brought them into being will also be responsible for their demise. It is important to keep in mind that they have never been really wealthy. This is something that should not be forgotten. A record of the private lives of the majority of the members of this class will demonstrate that they have genuinely been the most despicable and miserable of the impoverished.

The riches that may be attained by competitive means can never be said to be lasting or satisfying. They belong to you now, but someone else will take them tomorrow. Keep in mind that if you want to become wealthy through a method that is both scientific and certain, you have to get completely rid of the mindset of competing with others. You must never, ever, ever even consider the possibility that there is a finite amount available.

The instant you begin to believe that all of the money is being "cornered" and controlled by bankers and other individuals and that you must push yourself in order to have legislation enacted in order to halt this process, you have crossed over into the competitive state of mind. Your ability to bring about creativity will momentarily be taken away from you, and what is even worse is that you will most likely be unable to continue the creative processes that you have already started.

Be aware that the mountains of the earth contain unknown gold reserves worth tens of millions of dollars, hundreds of millions of dollars, and even billions of dollars.

Be aware that if there were not already enough of the thinking stuff, then more would be made to meet your requirements. Have faith that the money you need will come to you, even if it takes one thousand individuals to be guided to the discovery of fresh gold mines the day after tomorrow.

Always keep your focus on the infinite riches contained inside the formless substance rather than the apparent supply, and keep in mind that these riches are arriving to you at the same rate that you are able to take them in and put them to use. No one can prohibit you from acquiring what is rightfully yours, even if they control the whole visible supply. When you are ready to construct your home, you should never for one second entertain the thought that all of the prime building sites will already be occupied by other structures. Never feel frightened or worried about the trusts and combines because you are afraid that they may soon come to own the entire world.

You should never worry that you may miss out on anything you desire because another person "beats you to it." since there is no way that this could ever happen. You are not after something that is held by someone else; rather, you are working to bring into existence, out of the formless material, the thing that it is that you want. In addition to this, there is an infinite supply. Be true to the following articulated statement: There is a thinking substance from which all things are produced and which, in its original condition, pervades, penetrates, and fills the interspaces of the cosmos. The manifestation of the object that is envisioned by thought in this material is caused by a thought. A person is able to construct things in his thoughts, and then, by impressing those thoughts into formless matter, he may bring about the creation of the things he thinks about.

HOW IT IS THAT MONEY COMES TO YOU

When I tell you that you do not need to drive sharp bargains, I do not mean that you do not need to drive any bargains at all or that you are above the necessity of having any dealings with other people. What I mean when I say that you do not need to drive sharp bargains is that you do not have to drive sharp bargains.

It will not be necessary for you to deal with them in an unjust manner; you will not be required to get anything for free. You are able to offer more to each individual than what you receive from them. It is not possible to offer someone more in terms of monetary worth than you take from them, but it is possible to give them more in terms of the value they may get from the object you take from them.

There is a possibility that the book's paper, ink, and other components do not merit the price that you paid for it. Yet, if the suggestions in this book help you make thousands of dollars, the people who sold it to you did not commit any kind of fraud against you. They have provided you with a high worth of use for a relatively little monetary investment.

PROVIDING VALUE IN BUSINESS DEALINGS

Let us imagine that I am the owner of a painting that, in any civilized culture, would fetch a price of several thousand dollars. I take it to Baffin Bay, where I use my "salesmanship" skills to convince an Eskimo that he should trade it for a bundle of furs valued at five hundred dollars. I have done him a great disservice by giving him the photo when he has no need for it. That is useless to him, and it will not improve his quality of life in any way.

Now let us say that in exchange for his furs, I offer him a rifle that is worth $50. Then he successfully struck a reasonable deal. He has a need for the rifle; with it, he can get more furs and a great deal of food; it will improve his quality of life overall, and it will lead to his being wealthy.

As you go up from the level of competition to the level of creativity, you are able to examine your commercial dealings with a much more critical eye.

If you are selling something to a person and you see that it does not improve his life in any way beyond what he offers you in return, you have the right and the ability to cease the transaction. In order to succeed in business, you do not need to compete against anybody. And if you are working in an industry that is known to mistreat its employees, you need to find another line of work immediately.

Provide more in terms of use value to each individual than you receive from them in terms of financial worth. If this is the case, then each time you do business, you are contributing to the continued existence of the globe.

If you have employees working for you, you have a responsibility to extract more monetary value from them than they are paid in salary. You, however, have the ability to structure your company in such a way that it will be permeated with the idea of progression. So, any worker who is interested in advancing may do so incrementally on a daily basis if they so want.

You can make your company do for your workers what this book is doing for you by following the advice included inside it. You have the ability to run your company in such a way that it will serve as a stepping stone to financial success for each and every willing employee. And if he decides not to take advantage of the possibility, it is not your fault.

MANIFESTING SUCCESS

Even though you have the ability to coax your wealth out of the shapeless substance that permeates all of your surroundings, it does not necessarily follow that your good fortune will immediately take form from the air around you and materialize right in front of your very eyes once you have caused it to emerge from the void.

For example, if you want a sewing machine, I would suggest that before you impress the thought of a sewing machine on the thinking substance, you should first make sure that the image of the machine is clearly formed in your mind. Only then should you attempt to impress the thought of a sewing machine on the thinking substance. Hold the mental picture of a sewing machine in your mind with the greatest certain assurance that it is either being produced for you or is on its way to you if that is what you want. After having the notion for the first time, you should have the utmost certainty and unwavering conviction that the sewing machine will arrive soon. Never think about it or talk about it until you are certain that you already have it in your possession. Make the claim that it already belongs to you.

You shall get it by the might of the highest intellect, which will operate upon the minds of humanity. If you reside in Maine, it is possible that a person from Texas or Japan will be transported to your state so that they might participate in a transaction that will result in you obtaining what it is that you desire. If this is the case, the entire situation will work out to that person's benefit just as much as it does to yours.

Do not for a second lose sight of the fact that the thinking substance permeates everything, shares its experiences with everything, and has the power to affect everything. The thinking substance's need for more life and a higher quality of life has been responsible for the development of every sewing machine that has ever been manufactured, and it has the potential to be responsible for the development of millions more. It will do so once individuals put it into action by desiring it and having trust in it while also behaving in a certain manner.

A sewing machine is not out of the question for you to have in your home. You are free to acquire everything you like so long as you put it to work, improving not just your own life but also the lives of others around you.

You should not feel uncomfortable asking a lot of questions. Jesus said, "It is your Father's pleasure to give you the kingdom,"

The original essence wants to exist in you to the fullest extent possible; it wishes for you to have all that you are capable of or will need in order to lead the richest existence conceivable.

If you can impress onto your awareness the idea that the desire you have for the acquisition of wealth is identical to the desire of the Ultimate Power for a full manifestation of itself, then your faith will be unshakeable and unconquerable.

When I was younger, I once saw a little kid sitting at a piano and unsuccessfully attempting to coax harmony out of the keys.

I could see that his inability to play actual music was very frustrating and upsetting to him. When I asked him what was wrong, he said, "I can feel the music in me, but I can't make my hands go right." I was perplexed by his response, but I decided to let it go. The drive of the Original Substance to express itself through him was music, and it included all of the potentialities of all life. The kid was the conduit through which the whole of music sought its own manifestation.

Through humans, God, who is the One Substance, is attempting to live, act, and experience delight in the world. He is saying, "I want for my hands the ability to create wondrous constructions, to play heavenly harmonies, and to paint gorgeous images. I want to have feet so that I can do errands, eyes so that I can see the beauty that surrounds me, tongues so that I may speak powerful truths and sing magnificent melodies."

To the extent that anything is conceivable, it can only be expressed via human beings. God desires for people who have the ability to perform music to have access to the instruments they need and the tools to develop their skills to the utmost degree possible. He desires individuals who are capable of appreciating beauty to have the opportunity to surround themselves with things that are lovely. He desires that individuals who are able to recognize lies be provided with many opportunities to explore the world and gain new perspectives. Those who are able to enjoy fine clothing should have access to exquisite attire, and those who are able to appreciate delicious food should be lavishly nourished.

He desires all of these things because he takes pleasure in them and acknowledges their value. God is the one who longs to dance and sing, to revel in the splendor of creation, to share the truth, to dress elegantly, and to enjoy delicious cuisine.

Paul declared, "It is God that worketh in you to will and to do," and this is exactly what he meant.

The yearning for wealth that you have is the Infinite looking for an outlet of expression in you, just as he looked for an outlet of expression in the little child playing the piano.

You should not be afraid to ask a lot of questions. Your job is to zero in on and articulates the will of God in this situation.

The majority of individuals find this to be a challenging point. They still hold on to certain vestiges of the outdated notion that appeasing God requires a life of austerity and sacrifice. They consider destitution to be preordained by God and an inherent feature of the natural world. They are under the impression that God has completed his job and produced all of the things that he is able to provide and that the vast majority of humanity must continue to live in poverty because there is not enough to go around. Since so many people continue to believe this fallacy, it makes them uncomfortable to seek financial assistance. They make an effort not to demand anything more than a very modest level of skill, which is just enough to allow them to feel quite comfortable.

Now, I am thinking back on the experience of one student to whom it was explained that he needed to have a very specific mental image of the things he wanted in order for his imaginative thoughts about those things to be imprinted on the formless material. He had nothing more than the money he made from day to day, and he resided in a home that he leased out. He was a very poor guy.

He was unable to comprehend the idea that all money belonged to him. As a result, after giving the situation some thought, he came to the conclusion that it would be reasonable for him to request a new rug for the floor of his finest room as well as an anthracite coal stove to heat the home when the weather turns cold. After a few months, he was able to attain these goods by carefully following the directions provided in this book.

The realization hit him then that he had not inquired enough into the matter. He walked over to the home that he lived in and made a plan for all of the changes that he wanted to make to it in the future.

He envisioned a bay window here and a room there being constructed in his mind. He did not stop working on it until he had the impression that it had become his perfect house. And after that, he developed the interior decor of it.

He started living his life in a certain manner and making progress toward what it was that he desired while keeping the big picture in his mind. He just purchased the property and is renovating it to reflect the idea he has in his head of how he wants it to look. Today, with even more trust than before, he is moving forward to get even bigger things. It has been given to him in accordance with the faith he had, and the same is true for you and for all of us.

GRATITUDE

The examples that were provided in the previous chapter should have made it clear to the reader that the first step toward achieving financial success is to communicate the concept of what it is that you want to the formless material.

This is correct, and you will see that in order to achieve this goal, it is vital to establish a harmonious relationship between yourself and the formless intellect.

In light of the fact that maintaining this harmonic connection is a matter of such fundamental and critical significance, I shall devote part of this space to the discussion of it here. I will offer you instructions that, if you follow them, will unquestionably bring you into complete mental harmony with God. All you need to do is pay attention to what I say.

One word may adequately describe the whole of the mental adjustment and attunement process, and that word is thankfulness.

Initially, you hold the belief that there is a single intelligent substance that serves as the origin of all things. Second, you have the misconception that this drug would fulfill all of your needs and wishes. And thirdly, you connect to it by experiencing a sense of thankfulness that is both profound and very deep inside you.

In spite of the fact that they have their life in order in every other way, a great number of individuals remain impoverished due to a lack of gratitude. After receiving one gift from God, they chose not to acknowledge him in any way, so severing the connection that they had with him.

It is not hard to comprehend that the riches we amass will increase in proportion to our proximity to the original source of that wealth. It is simple to comprehend that a soul that is always appreciative lives in a state of existence that is more in tune with God than a soul that never acknowledges God's existence by means of gratitude.

The more gratefully we focus our thoughts on the Ultimate Power when wonderful things happen to us, the more good things will come to us in the future, and the more quickly they will arrive. The explanation for this is straightforwardly due to the fact that cultivating an attitude of appreciation in one's thinking brings one's consciousness into closer proximity with the origin of one's blessings.

If the idea that being grateful puts your whole mind into greater harmony with the creative energy of the universe is one that you have not previously considered, give it some careful consideration, and you will discover that it is true. Because of compliance with certain rules, you already have access to a number of beneficial resources. Your thoughts will naturally wander out along the paths from which things originate when you are grateful. Also, it will help you maintain a tight harmony with creative thinking and prevent you from sliding into the trap of a competitive mind.

Just having an attitude of gratitude may keep you focused on the infinite and prevent you from making the mistake of believing that there is a finite amount of wealth available, which is a belief that would be disastrous for your ambitions and dreams.

There is a principle known as the law of thankfulness, and in order for you to get the outcomes that you want, it is imperative that you comply with this principle.

The natural principle that states that action and response are always equal and go in opposite directions is known as the "law of gratitude." The release of your mind's energy in the form of grateful praise sent to the Highest Power is an expenditure of power; it cannot fail to reach the target to which it is directed since it is an expression of gratitude. And as a direct consequence of this, God reacts by immediately moving closer to you in his presence.

"Draw nigh unto God, and He will draw nigh unto you." It is an observation that is true from a psychological standpoint.

In addition, the response in the formless material will be powerful and consistent if your thankfulness is of a strong and consistent kind. The direction of travel for the things that you desire will always be in your direction. See how Jesus constantly seemed to be expressing his gratitude to the Father by saying, "I thank Thee, Father, that Thou hearest me." (I thank Thee, Father that Thou hearest me) Since appreciation is what maintains your connection to power, it is impossible to exert much force if you lack thankfulness.

But, the significance of appreciation does not rely exclusively upon the prospect of acquiring further benefits in the foreseeable future. Without an attitude of thankfulness, it is impossible to avoid becoming discontent with the way things now are.

As soon as you give your mind permission to ruminate in a dissatisfied manner on the current state of affairs, you will start to lose ground. You focus your attention on what is common, poor, dirty, and mean, and as a result, your mind takes on the shape of these characteristics. After that, you will send these forms or mental representations to the place where there is no form. Because of this, you may expect the common, the poor, the dirty, and the mean to approach you.

When you let your thoughts wander to things that are beneath you, you not only bring inferiority upon yourself but also surround yourself with things that are beneath you. On the other side, if you focus your attention on the greatest, you will attract more of the best into your life, and you will become the best yourself.

The creative force that is inside each of us transforms us into an image of whatever we focus our attention on. We are now engaging in thinking of substance, and thinking always results in the formation of the thing that it thinks about.

The mentality that is thankful is one that is always focused on the very best. Because of this, it has the potential to become the best; it assumes the nature or qualities of the greatest, and as a result, it will be given the best.

Also, appreciation is the mother of faith. The appreciative mind anticipates pleasant things on a constant basis, and this anticipation transforms into faith. Faith is produced when there is an attitude of thankfulness toward one's own intellect. Faith is increased with each successive wave of gratitude and appreciation that is sent. A person who does not have a sense of thankfulness cannot keep a live faith for a lengthy period of time. And as we shall see in the chapters that follow, you cannot become wealthy via the creative approach if you do not have faith that it is alive and well.

It is vital, then, to make it a practice of constantly expressing gratitude for anything good that happens to you and to create an attitude of gratitude for everything good that comes your way. And since everything has a hand in your progress, you should not leave anything out of your expression of thankfulness because it is all a part of your success.

It is a waste of time to dwell on the failings or wrongdoings of trust magnates or plutocrats, either in your thoughts or in conversation. Your chance has been created as a result of their organizing of the planet. All that has been given to you could not have been possible without their help.

Do not rage against crooked politicians. Your opportunities would be significantly reduced if there were no politicians to keep order in what would otherwise be a chaotic society.

To get us to this point in terms of business and government, God has been working tirelessly and with an incredible amount of patience. And he is carrying on with his job in the same manner. I have no doubt that he will eliminate plutocrats, trust magnates, captains of industry, and politicians as soon as he has the opportunity to do so. In the interim, though, they are an absolute must. It is important to keep in mind that they are assisting in the process of arranging the transmission lines down which your wealth will arrive to you. Show your gratitude to them. This will put you into a harmonic connection with the good in everything, and goodwill will gravitate toward you as a result of this.

THE ART OF THINKING IN A CERTAIN WAY

If you reread the tale of the guy who created a mental picture of his home, you will have a better understanding of the first step that must be taken in order to become wealthy. You need to have a crystal-clear and unmistakable mental image of what it is that you desire. You cannot communicate an idea to someone else unless you have that notion yourself.

Before you can offer it to someone else, you need to have it yourself. And a lot of individuals are not able to impress the thinking substance because they just have a fuzzy and hazy idea of the things they desire to achieve, have, or become for themselves.

It is not sufficient to have a broad desire for riches "to do good with." You must also have specific goals. The aspiration is shared by everybody.

It is not enough to just have the desire to travel, see things, live more, or anything else along those lines. They are aspirations shared by every single person.

If you were to send a buddy a telegraph message, you would not transmit the letters of the alphabet in the sequence in which they appear and then allow your friend to figure out what the message means on his own, would you? You also would not choose terms at random from the dictionary, would you? You would send a statement that made sense and meant something to the recipient.

Remember that in order to convey your desires to the thinking substance, you will need to do it in a way that is logically consistent with what you are saying. You need to have a clear idea of what it is that you desire.

Sending out unformed longings and wants is a certain way to ensure that you will never get wealthy or set the wheels of creative force in motion.

Examine your wants and needs in the same manner that I described the guy doing with his home. Understand clearly what it is that you desire and form a distinct mental image of how you would want it to seem after you have achieved it.

You need to always have a clear mental image in your head, much as a sailor always has the destination that he is headed for in his head as they sail toward it. You are required to keep your gaze fixed on it at all times. It is not essential to do exercises in concentration, to set apart particular periods for prayer and affirmation, to "go into the silence," nor to perform occult tricks of any sort. You must not lose sight of it any more than the steersman loses sight of the compass. These things are fine, but what you really need is to be aware of what it is that you want and to have a strong enough desire for it to keep it in the forefront of your mind.

Consider your photo in as much of your spare time as you possibly can. This will help you appreciate it more. Keep in mind that one does not need to do any specific exercises in order to focus their thoughts on something that one really wants. It takes more work to pay attention to things that are not truly important to you since you do not care as much about them.

If your desire to become wealthy is not strong enough to keep your thoughts focused on the goal, in the same way, that the magnetic pole of a compass keeps the needle pointing in the correct direction, then it will not be worth your time to attempt to put the advice in this book into practice.

Those whose desire for money is strong enough to overcome mental lethargy and the love of ease are the target audience for the solutions that I will provide in this section.

Your desire will become more intense if you concentrate on painting an accurate and specific image of what you want and if you give it more thought and attention. And the more intense your desire is, the simpler it will be to keep your attention riveted on the mental image of the thing you want it to be.

Nevertheless, just having a good vision of the big picture is not enough; something more is required. If that is the only thing you do, you are nothing more than a dreamer, and you will have very little or no ability to really do anything. Your well-defined objective should be backed up by the intention to make it a reality and make it manifest in some kind of expression. In addition, you need to have an unshakeable and unflinching confidence that the object in question is already yours, that it is close at hand, and that all that is required of you is to claim ownership of it.

Maintain a mental presence in the new home while the construction of the actual structure continues. In the sphere of the mind, immediately immerse yourself in the complete pleasure of the things you want.

Jesus told his disciples, "Whatsoever things ye ask for when ye pray, believe that ye receive them, and ye shall have them,"

Imagine that the things you desire are already in your possession and that you are making full use of them. See yourself as the owner of these things and in the process of utilizing them. You should put them to use in your mind in the same way that you would put them to use when you really get possession of them. Focus your attention on the image in your head until it becomes crystal clear. The next step is to adopt a mental stance of ownership toward everything that is shown in the image. Imagine that you own it and do so with the conviction that it really is yours. Take mental ownership of it. Maintain this mental ownership; the conviction that it is genuine should not waver for even a second as you go about your day.

Furthermore, keep in mind what was said in previous chapters on gratitude: show the same level of appreciation for it now as you anticipate feeling after it has fully materialized. Real faith may be shown in a person when they are able to honestly thank God for things that they only possess in their thoughts. That individual will become wealthy, and that person will be able to bring into existence whatever else he desires.

There is no need for you to pray again and over again for the things that you want. It is not required that you inform God of it each and every day. "Use not vain repetitions as the heathen do," Jesus instructed his students, "for your Father knoweth that ye have need of these things before ye ask Him." This was in contrast to the practice of the pagan peoples of the time.

Your job is to articulate your desire in an educated manner for the things that make for a fuller existence and to have these wishes ordered into a logical whole. This will be your contribution. The next step is to communicate your whole desire to the formless substance, which has both the capability and the motivation to grant your want.

You do not create this impression by reciting a string of words; rather, you create this impact by holding the vision with the unwavering intent to achieve it and with the unwavering trust that you will achieve it.

It is not according to your faith while you are talking about your faith that the answer to prayer will be given to you; rather, it will be given to you according to your faith while you are working.

You will not be able to sway God's will by telling him what you want on the Sabbath and then ignoring him the other six days of the week. This is because the Sabbath is God's day of rest. If you do not think about your prayer until the next time the hour of prayer rolls around, it will not matter how many special times you set apart to go into your room and pray because he will not be impressed.

Although verbal prayer may help you see more clearly and build your faith, it will not be your verbal prayers that bring you what you desire in the end. You do not need a "sweet hour of prayer." in order to achieve financial success. It is imperative that you "pray without ceasing." And by prayer, I mean clinging tenaciously to your vision with the intention of bringing about its materialization and the conviction that you are in the process of accomplishing this goal.

"Believe that ye receive them."

After you have a distinct picture in your mind of what you want, the next step is to practice receiving. After you have it formulated, it is a good idea to make an oral declaration by addressing the Highest Power in respectful prayer. This should be done as soon as possible. From that point on, you have to train your mind to accept what it is that you are asking for. You should live in the new home, wear good clothing, ride in the vehicle, go on the trip, and confidently prepare for ever more extensive trips.

Consider and discuss all of the things you have requested in terms of real ownership at the current time. Envision the precise environment and financial situation that you want, and then try to live your life as if you already had it.

This will help you get closer to achieving your goals. Take note, however, that you are not engaging in this activity in the capacity of a simple daydreamer and castle constructor. Maintain both your confidence that the unreal is becoming real and your focus on the goal that must be accomplished in order to make it so.

Keep in mind that the difference between a scientist and a dreamer is trust and purpose in the use of their imagination. This is what sets the dreamer apart from the scientist. And now that you are aware of this reality, you must come to this place to learn how to make effective use of your will.

HOW TO USE THE WILL

If you want to get wealthy through a method that is supported by science, you should avoid directing your willpower toward anything that is located outside of yourself.

You have no authority to act in such a manner, regardless. It is unethical to impose one's will on the bodies of other people in order to coerce them into doing an action that one desires.

It is just as morally repugnant and immoral to compel someone with mental power as it is to coerce them through physical strength. If forcing people to do things for you by using physical force brings them to a state of slavery, then using mental coercion to force people to do things for you achieves the exact same result. The two approaches are solely distinguishable in their methodology. If stealing things from other people by using physical force is robbery, then using mental coercion to take things also constitutes robbery. In theory, there is no distinction between the two.

You have no authority to impose your will on another person, even if you are saying it is "for his own good," since you do not know what is in that person's best interest.

The science of being wealthy does not need you to use power or coercion over any other individual in any manner, shape, or form under any circumstance. There is not the tiniest bit of justification for acting in this manner. In point of fact, any effort to impose your will on other people would almost certainly result in the failure of your plan.

It is not necessary to exert your willpower in order for things to come to you; they will come to you anyway. It would amount to nothing more than an attempt to force God's will, and it would be both silly and pointless, as well as blasphemous.

You do not need to use your willpower to coerce God into giving you wonderful things any more than you need to use your might to force the sun to rise in the morning. You do not need to utilize your willpower to subdue a hostile deity or to make obstinate and defiant forces perform what you want them to.

The thinking material is pleasant to interact with and is more eager to give you what you desire than you are to get it.

Just applying your willpower to yourself is all that is required to achieve financial success.

When you are aware of what you should be thinking and doing, you have to utilize your willpower to force yourself to think and act in the appropriate manner. That is the correct way to make use of your willpower in order to obtain what you desire, and that is to utilize it in order to keep yourself on the right path. Make use of your willpower to ensure that you continue to think and behave in a predetermined manner.

Do not attempt to impose your will, your ideas, or your state of mind on other entities or people by sending them into space. Keep your thoughts in the house. There, it is able to achieve more than in any other location.

Make use of your intellect to create a mental picture of what it is that you desire, and then keep that vision in your mind while maintaining your faith and your purpose. Make use of your willpower to keep your thoughts operating in the appropriate manner.

Since you will leave only good impacts on formless stuff, the speed with which you amass wealth is directly proportional to the steadiness and consistency with which you pursue your faith and mission. You will not be able to cancel them out or compensate for them with bad ones.

The formless material takes in an image of your wants and permits this picture to permeate it to huge distances—possibly all the way to the cosmos.

The more widespread this perception becomes, the more things begin to move in the direction of its actualization. All living things, all inanimate things, and even those that have not yet been formed are being influenced in the direction of bringing into existence what it is that you desire. The application of all forces immediately shifts in that direction. Everything will start moving in your direction. People all around the world have their thoughts changed to the point where they will do whatever it takes to help you achieve your goals. And you do not even realize they are helping you.

All of this, however, may be verified by first establishing a negative impression of the formless material. It is just as certain to start a movement away from you when you have doubt or unbelief as it is to start a movement toward you when you have trust and purpose. Since they lack knowledge of this, the majority of individuals are doomed to failure when they attempt to apply "mental science" to amass wealth. Every hour and every minute that you spend paying regard to your uncertainties and concerns, every hour that you spend worrying, every hour that your soul is captivated by unbelief—all of these things set a current away from you across the whole of the intelligent substance's dominion. "All the promises are unto them that believe, and unto them only." the Bible says. Take note of how adamant Jesus was about this particular topic of doctrine. You are now aware of the cause behind this.

Because belief is everything, it is in your best interest to keep watch on your thoughts. And since the things that you notice and think about will play a significant role in the formation of your beliefs, it is essential that you direct your attention in a certain direction. The will comes into play in this situation because it is through the application of the will that you choose the things to which you will give your attention.

If you want to become wealthy, you should not educate yourself on what it is like to be poor. Thinking about the things' antitheses does not result in the creation of those things. It is never possible to improve one's health by learning about sickness or dwelling on it in one's thoughts. Sin and thoughts about sin are not topics that should be studied in an effort to advance righteousness. Studying the poor and dwelling on their plight has never resulted in financial success for anybody.

The field of medicine, which studies diseases, has contributed to the spread of certain diseases. Sin has been encouraged by religion since religion is a science of sin. And economics, as the study of poverty, will make the world a more miserable and impoverished place to live in.

Do not bring up the subject of poverty. You should not look into it, and you should not worry about it. Never mind trying to figure out what caused it. You are in no way connected to them in any way. What is important to you is finding a solution.

Spending your time participating in philanthropic activity or charitable initiatives is not recommended. Charity, in whatever form, has the unavoidable tendency to contribute to the same misery that it purports to alleviate.

I am not suggesting that you should have a callous heart or be rude to others, nor am I suggesting that you should ignore pleas for help. Therefore, you should not make any attempt to reduce poverty through any of the conventional methods. Put an end to your history of poverty and all associated with it, and "make good." in your life.

If you constantly flood your mind with images of destitution, it will be impossible for you to maintain the mental picture that is required to make you wealthy. Do not read any books or periodicals that describe the wretchedness of tenement residents or the horrors of child labor. This will only serve to depress and upset you. Avoid reading anything that may bring depressing thoughts of need and anguish into your head, such as novels or newspapers. If you are aware of these facts, you will not be able to assist the needy in any way. The general awareness of the conditions that the poor are living in does not in any way contribute to the eradication of poverty. It is not helpful to fill one's head with images of poverty; rather, it is more effective to fill the heads of the poor with images of prosperity. This has a greater tendency to eradicate poverty.

When you choose not to let your thoughts be flooded with images of other people's suffering, you are not abandoning those who are impoverished in their plight in any way.

There is a route out of poverty, and it is not by increasing the number of wealthy people who think about poverty; rather, it is by growing the number of impoverished people who, through the application of faith and purpose, are successful in climbing out of poverty and becoming wealthy.

Charity is not necessary for those who are destitute. They are in need of being inspired. The only thing that charity does for them is sending them a loaf of bread to eat so that they may continue to exist in their destitution or provide them with some kind of amusement so that they can forget about it for an hour or two. They will, however, be lifted out of their suffering by a source of inspiration. If you wish to assist others who are less fortunate, you should show them that it is possible for them to become wealthy by being wealthy yourself. Become wealthy. This is the most effective approach for you to assist others who are less fortunate.

The only way that poverty can ever be eradicated from our planet is if a significant number of people, a number that is steadily growing, put the advice in this book into practice.

Individuals need to be educated that the path to financial success is creativity, not competition.

Every individual who climbs to wealth via the process of competition brings others with them and knocks down the ladder on which they climb. But, every individual who becomes wealthy through their own creative endeavors paves the path for thousands of others to follow in his footsteps and encourages others to do so. When you choose not to have sympathy for people in need, contemplate or speak about those in need, or listen to others who do so, you are not displaying a callous or unfeeling disposition. Nor are you demonstrating a hardness of heart or an unfeeling disposition. Make use of your self-control to keep your thoughts off of being poor and instead keep them set, with faith and purpose, on the vision of what it is that you want to achieve.

FURTHER USE OF THE WILL

If you are constantly diverting your attention to competing images, whether they are real or imagined, you will not be able to keep a genuine and unclouded picture of riches in your mind.

Do not let anyone know about any previous financial difficulties. Avoid thinking about them under any circumstances. Do not let anybody know about the financial struggles that you had as a child or the impoverished state of your parents. If you do any of these things, you are psychologically placing yourself in the category of the impoverished for the time being, and this will most definitely slow down the progression of things toward you.

Jesus reportedly remarked, "Let the dead bury their dead," and we paraphrase him here.

Put all aspects of poverty and being poor, including poverty itself, fully in the past.

You have decided that a certain hypothesis about the world must be true because you have placed all of your faith in it and believe that only if it is true will you be happy. What do you stand to gain by giving consideration to competing theories?

Do not read any religious literature that warns you that the end of the world is near or that it is already here. Do not waste your time reading the works of muckrakers and other gloomy thinkers who will tell you that it is heading in the direction of the devil. The fate of the world is not in the hands of the devil. It will be presented to God. That is fantastic coming into being.

It is possible that the current state of affairs has a great number of elements that are unfavorable. So, what is the use of studying them when it is clear that they are fading away and when their research of them simply tries to check their passing and keep them with us? Why spend time and attention on things that are going to be eliminated as a result of evolutionary development when the only way you can speed up their removal is by boosting evolutionary growth to the extent that your contribution to it goes?

If you even entertain the possibility of going to particular nations, regions, or locations, you are squandering your time and lowering your chances of success. This is true regardless of how terrible the circumstances may seem to be. You should get interested in how the wealth of the world is increasing.

Instead of focusing on the squalor that the globe is emerging from, try to picture the wealth that is soon to be its reality. Furthermore, keep in mind that the only way you can aid the world in becoming richer is by growing wealthy yourself using the creative technique rather than the competitive one. This is the only way you can contribute to the growth of wealth in the world.

Pay exclusive attention to wealth and completely disregard a lack of it. When you think about or talk of people who are poor, you should think and speak of them as those who are becoming wealthy - as individuals who are to be praised rather than pitied. This should be done whenever you are thinking about or speaking about those who are poor. They, along with other people, will then get inspired and start looking for a way out of the situation.

If I tell you that you should devote all your attention, time, and thoughts to acquiring wealth, it does not necessarily follow that you should behave in a sleazy or impolite manner.

To achieve true wealth is the most admirable goal one can have in life since doing so encompasses all other accomplishments.

When we enter the creative mind, everything is different than when we are operating on the competitive plane. On the competitive plane, the fight to acquire wealth is a godless race for control over other people.

Becoming wealthy is the path that leads to all of the possibilities for grandeur and the unfolding of one's soul, for acts of service, and for endeavors of the highest kind. The application of things is what makes anything feasible.

If you do not already possess physical health, you will discover that achieving such health is contingent on your financial success. Those who are free from the stress of financial concerns, who have the resources to live a carefree living, and who adhere to sanitary habits are the only ones who can achieve and maintain a healthy state.

Those who are able to rise beyond the struggle for existence as a competitive struggle are the only ones who are capable of moral and spiritual grandeur. Indeed, the only people who are exempt from the degrading forces of rivalry are those who are growing wealthy on the level of creative thinking. Keeping in mind that love blossoms most beautifully in environments that are characterized by refinement, a high level of thinking, and independence from forces that might corrupt, it is important if you have the goal of achieving home bliss. They are only to be found in places where wealth may be acquired via the application of creative intellect in the absence of competition or warfare.

I will say it again: there is no greater or more admirable goal than to get wealthy. You have to force yourself to ignore everything else, even anything that can make your vision cloudy or dull, and concentrate only on the image of wealth that you have in your head.

You need to have the ability to see the fundamental truth that lies underneath everything. You have to be able to discern the great one life that is ever moving ahead toward broader expression and complete enjoyment underlying any conditions that may seem to be going wrong.

There is no such thing as poverty, and this is a fact that cannot be refuted.

The only thing that exists is riches. Some individuals may not realize that there are riches waiting for them, and as a result, they choose to continue living in poverty. The most effective method for educating these individuals is to demonstrate to them, through your own life and practice, how one may achieve financial success. Others remain impoverished despite the fact that they are aware of the existence of a route out of their situation; yet, they are incapable of exerting the level of mental effort required to locate and follow that route. And the absolute greatest thing you can do for these individuals is to pique their interest by demonstrating to them the joy that can be attained via having an appropriate amount of wealth.

Others are impoverished because, despite the fact that they have some understanding of scientific principles, they have gotten so bogged down and disoriented in a labyrinth of occult and metaphysical ideas that they do not know which path to choose. They experiment with a variety of different systems, all of which end in failure. Again, the absolute greatest thing that you can do in this regard is to demonstrate to them in your own life and work out how things need to be done. The value of theory can never compare to the power of actual experience.

Your contribution to the world will be greatly enhanced if you focus on developing yourself to your full potential.

Becoming wealthy is the single most effective method for you to serve God and your fellow people. There is no other option. That is, provided that you amass your wealth by imaginative means rather than through aggressive ones.

Furthermore, one more thing. I believe that this book explains, in great depth, the fundamentals of the scientific approach to amassing wealth. There is no other book on the topic that you should read at this time. This may come out as exclusive and self-centered. Addition, subtraction, multiplication, and division are the only four operations in mathematics that may be considered scientifically accurate as methods of computing. There is no alternative approach that can be used. There is no way for there to be more than one route, that is, the shortest distance between two places.

Thinking scientifically can only be done in one way, and that is in a manner that seeks to get to one's destination in the quickest and least complicated manner possible.

Nobody has ever come up with a method that is either simpler or more condensed than the one I am going to describe right now. It has had everything that is not necessarily removed from it. After you start using this strategy, you should stop using any others. Leave them completely out of your mind and move on.

Read this book on a daily basis. Keep it close at hand. Remember it as best you can. Avoid considering the validity of any other frameworks or ideas. If you do that, you will start to have second thoughts, you will feel hesitant, and your thinking process will fluctuate. If this is the case, you will introduce the unfavorable idea into the formless material.

When you have achieved success and grown wealthy, you are free to devote as much time as you want to the study of various methodologies.

Do not read anything further on this topic than the works of the writers who are named in the introduction until you are absolutely certain that you have achieved what it is that you set out to do.

You should only read the most upbeat responses to the most recent global news; focus on remarks that fit in with your overall perspective.

You should also put off any inquiries into the occult for the time being. Never become involved with theosophy, spiritualism, or kindred subjects; they are all dangerous. It is quite probable that the deceased continue to exist and are located nearby. But if that is the case, you should leave them alone. Get your nose out of my business.

No matter where the souls of the deceased may be, they still have their own tasks to do and issues that need to be resolved.

We have no authority to intervene in what they are doing. They are beyond our ability to aid. It is quite unlikely that they will be able to assist us, and even if they can, it is questionable whether or not we have the authority to encroach on their time. The living should leave the deceased and the afterlife alone. Find a solution to your own difficulty; increase your wealth. If you start dabbling in the occult, mental crosscurrents will begin to run through your head, and they will eventually lead to the demise of your aspirations.

In conclusion, both this chapter and the ones that came before it has led us to the following assertion of fundamental truths:

There is a thinking stuff from which all things are produced and which, in its unaltered state, pervades, penetrates, and fills the interspaces of the world. All things are made of this thinking stuff.

The manifestation of the item that is envisaged by thought in this material is produced by the idea itself.

A person is able to construct things in his thoughts, and then, by impressing those thoughts into formless matter, he may bring about the creation of the things he thinks about.

In order to do this, a person's mindset has to shift from one of competition to one of creativity. It is necessary for him to have a crystal clear mental image of the things that he desires. And, he must keep this picture in his thoughts with the steadfast purpose to get what he wants and the unwavering faith that he will get what he wants—closing his mind against all that may tend to shake his purpose, dim his vision, or quench his faith. And he must keep this picture in his thoughts with the fixed purpose of getting what he wants and the unwavering faith that he will get what he wants.

In addition to all of this, we are going to observe now that he is required to live and behave in a certain manner.

ACTING IN THE CERTAIN WAY

The creative power is prodded into action by the impetus of thought. The right method of thinking will lead to financial success, but you can not only focus on your thoughts and ignore your actions. Many scientifically-informed metaphysicians run aground due to this fatal flaw in their thinking, which prevents them from translating their ideas into meaningful action.

We have not yet advanced to the point where one may make anything out of nothing, bypassing either the processes of nature or the labor of human hands. You can not just ponder and sit on the sidelines.

The riches hidden deep inside the mountains may be drawn to you just by focusing your thoughts on them. It won't, however, dig itself out of the ground, purify itself, mint itself into double eagles, and magically appear in your pocket as you go.

The Ultimate Power will direct the affairs of the people in such a way that someone will be compelled to mine the gold for you. Moreover, the gold will be delivered to you via the shrewd business dealings of a third party. You are responsible for setting up your own corporate affairs to allow for its arrival. Everything, living and nonliving, is at your command once you set your mind to it. Yet your behavior must be such that you are in a position to properly accept what you want when it arrives. Do not consider it charity or steal it. Every single individual must get more in-use value from you than he or she pays you in cash.

The scientific application of thinking is visualizing precisely what it is you desire, being steadfast in your determination to achieve your goal, and accepting the results of your efforts with gratitude and trust.

Do not use mystical or occult techniques to send your thoughts out into the world in the hopes that they will accomplish your goals. Spending time and energy on something like that is a waste of time and will impair your ability to think rationally.

The activity of the mind in acquiring wealth has been thoroughly described in the previous chapters. With your conviction and focus, you must leave a lasting impression on the lifeless matter, which shares your need for expansion. And this inspiration from you sends the creative forces into activity in their usual ways, but with you in mind.

You should not try to direct or oversee the imaginative process. Keep your focus, stay true to your mission, and never lose your faith or your sense of appreciation, and you will succeed.

But, there is a certain course of action you must do in order to claim what rightfully belongs to you; to embrace the elements of your vision and assign them their respective placements.

Insight into its veracity is not hard to get by. Whatever you want will first pass through the hands of others, who will then demand payment in exchange for it.

The only way to gain what is rightfully yours is to give the other person what is justly his.

Money will not magically appear in your wallet, and it will not stay full without any input from you.

In the science of becoming wealthy, the act of receiving is crucial since it is at this time that one must integrate their own ideas and efforts. Many people's powerful and persistent aspirations, whether conscious or unconscious, serve to activate their creative energies. They do not have the means to benefit from the arrival of what they want, though, so they stay impoverished.

Your thoughts are powerful enough to bring anything you need to you.

The only way to get it is to do something.

No matter what you decide to do, you need to take some kind of action immediately. There is nothing you can do to change the past.

Eliminating distractions and focusing only on the present is crucial for sharp thinking. The future is not now. Thus you cannot do anything about it. It is also impossible to know how you will feel or what you will do in a certain emergency situation until that time actually comes.

Do not put off taking action because you are not in the ideal business or setting at the moment. And do not waste the here and now strategizing the best way out of potential crises in the future. Do not doubt your own abilities to handle any sudden situation that may arise.

If you take action right now while thinking about what could happen later, you will not be fully present, and your efforts will fail. Focus completely on what you are doing right now.

Do not invest your creative energy into the source material and then wait for the desired outcomes to materialize; you will be disappointed. Take immediate action. Never has there been a better moment than now, and there never will be. The time to start preparing for the arrival of what you desire is now.

You can only take action on the people and things around you right now if you are doing it in the context of your current job or line of work.

You cannot do anything if you are not there. You cannot change what is in the past, and you cannot change what is in the future. You are limited to doing the action in the present moment.

Do not waste time thinking about how brilliantly or badly you performed yesterday. Be productive today.

Try not to worry about tomorrow's tasks today. It can be done in your spare time tomorrow.

Do not attempt to influence inaccessible individuals or events by the use of occult or mystical techniques.

To take action, you need not await a shift in circumstance. Make a conscious effort to alter your surroundings.

You have the power to alter your current setting in order to facilitate relocation to a more desirable location.

Keep your sights set on that better world you see for yourself, but take full use of the resources at your disposal right now.

Do not waste time fantasizing or constructing imaginary worlds. Keep your sights set on the end goal, and take immediate action.

Do not aimlessly search for a first step toward financial success by looking for something novel to try or something very extraordinary to accomplish. It is likely that your routine will remain mostly unchanged for some time.

But from now on, you will operate in a certain manner that will definitely lead to financial success.

Do not put off taking action if you are currently involved in a company you believe is not the correct one for you. You do not give up or wallow in self-pity just because you are in the wrong location.

No one has ever been so lost that he could not find his way, and no one has been so engrossed in the wrong line of work that he could not find his way into the proper line of work.

Have trust that you will succeed in the correct line of work, and keep seeing yourself there. But, take action in your current role. Utilize the resources at your disposal to pave the way to a brighter future. If you are in a bad environment now, use it to move into a better one later.

If you have trust in your vision of the ideal company and stay focused on your goal, the Highest Power will bring it to you. And if you do things in a certain manner, you will start heading in the direction of the company.

Do not depend on your wishful thinking to get you a new job if you are already employed and believe you must switch positions to achieve your goals. It is quite unlikely to succeed in its intended purpose.

If you can see yourself successfully employed in the position you want and then apply that same level of trust and determination to your current position, you will eventually get hired in that position.

Just believe, and the creative power will be activated to deliver it to you. More than that, however, your very own environment's forces will be influenced by your actions to push you in the direction of your goals. Now that we have reached the end of this section, I would like to add one last requirement to our course outline:

The initial state of the thinking substance that all things are built from pervades, penetrates and fills the voids of the cosmos.

Everything that can be imagined may be created by thought in this medium.

A person may shape an object in his mind and then bring it into existence by impressing his ideas on the amorphous matter.

To do this, one must make the mental leap from competitive to creative thinking. He has to create a concrete mental image of the outcomes he desires.

And he has to keep this image in his head with the determination to achieve his goals and the certainty that he will succeed, all the while blocking out everything that may make him doubt his abilities.

A person has to take use of the people and resources available to him right now so that he may be ready to obtain what he desires when the time comes.

EFFICIENT ACTION

It is essential that you use your mind in the ways I have shown in the preceding chapters as soon as you are able to, start doing what you can accomplish where you are, and keep doing that until you have exhausted your options.

Only by surpassing your current status can you go forward. And no individual is bigger than his current station if he fails to complete the duties associated with that station.

Only those who do more than their assigned tasks contribute to the world at large.

Many aspects of society would regress if his current position was not filled. Weakening society, government, commerce, and industry are those who do not fully fulfill their current roles. They need expensively being carried along by others. Those who have important positions but do not actively work to fill them slow global growth. They are remnants of a bygone era and a lower tier of existence. They are prone to deterioration. As social progress is regulated by the law of physical and mental evolution, no society could grow if every member was less than his station. An overabundance of life is the primary driver of evolution in the animal kingdom.

When an organism's vitality exceeds what can be represented via its own plane's functions, it evolves to acquire the requisite higher-plane organs, and a new species is born.

Without creatures that could more than fill their positions, new species would never have evolved. For your purposes, the legislation remains unaltered. You need to apply this approach to your own life if you want to become wealthy.

Each day brings either progress or setback. Because it is the good days that bring you where you are going, if you consistently experience setbacks, it will be impossible to amass great wealth. On the other hand, if you have success, you have no choice but to become wealthy.

If something can be done today, but you put it off until tomorrow, you will have failed at it. What is more, it is possible the repercussions may be far worse than you anticipate.

Not even the smallest action can be predicted to have no effect. There are forces at work on your behalf that you are unaware of. Any little action on your part might have far-reaching consequences; it could be the key that unlocks a world of possibility.

When it comes to the globe and human events, you can never know all the combinations that the Highest Power is crafting for you. If you do not accomplish one simple action, you might end up waiting a very long time for what you desire.

Attempt to do as much as you can each day.

But, there is a caveat that has to be taken into mind. In an endeavor to get the most work done in the least amount of time, you must not overwork or rush into your company without first carefully considering the implications of your actions.

You should not strive to do tasks that would normally take two days in one day or a week in one day.

Efficiency in what you do is more important than quantity.

A given action may be either effective or ineffective. Every ineffective action is a wasted opportunity, and a lifetime of such actions will lead to nothing but disappointment. If every action you do is ineffective, you will end up worse off as you multiply your efforts.

Yet, if you live a life in which every action you do is effective, then your whole existence must be a triumph.

Doing too much, inefficiently, or not enough at all is what ultimately leads to failure.

You will see that it is a no-brainer that being wealthy is a natural consequence of doing more productive things than wasteful ones. If you can find ways to maximize the effectiveness of your actions, you will be reminded that wealth creation is, at its core, a mathematical science.

The issue is whether or not you can ensure the success of each individual effort. This is something you are capable of.

Since Infinite is on your side, and Infinity can do nothing but succeed, you can guarantee the success of any endeavor you undertake.

If you need help, the Highest Power is at your disposal. All you need to do to make your actions count is put your own strength into them.

All actions are either powerful or weak. If you wait until everyone is powerful, then do the actions that are certain to make you wealthy.

Keeping your vision in mind while you take action and investing all of your faith and determination will make your efforts more powerful and fruitful.

Those who try to have mental strength without also having physical strength ultimately fail. They think in one location and at one moment and then do something else entirely in another. Their actions are not effective enough on their own. Hence they fail. Including the Highest Power in even the most routine actions, however, will make them all worthwhile. It is true that one triumph paves the path for future triumphs. In other words, both your forward mobility and the speed at which your goals are approaching will increase.

Keep in mind that the benefits of taking effective action build over time. When a man takes steps toward a more significant existence, more and more things latch onto him, amplifying the impact of his aspirations. This is so because every material object has an innate need to live.

Always give 100% of all you have got on any given day, and make sure everything you do counts.

While it is important to have your vision in mind at all times, this does not imply that you need to be able to make out every little aspect of it as you go about your day. During your downtime, you should visualize the finer points of your vision so that you may commit it to memory.

Spend almost all of your free time on this if you want to see fast results. Having a clear mental image of your goal, formed through prolonged reflection, will allow you to more easily convey that image to the mind of the shapeless material. So, while you are at work, all you have to do is think about the image to renew your sense of hope and dedication. Think about your image when you are not busy so that it becomes embedded in your mind and you can recognize it instinctively. You will become so enamored with the promising future that even thinking about it will fill you with a powerful surge of vitality.

Let us go through our course outline once again, but this time with updated closing remarks to reflect where we are today. The initial state of the thinking substance that all things are built from pervades, penetrates and fills the voids of the cosmos.

What you envision happens when you put your thoughts into this material.

A person may shape an object in his mind and then bring it into existence by impressing his thinking into the amorphous matter.

To do this, one must make the mental leap from competitive to creative thinking. He has to create a concrete mental image of the outcomes he desires. He must have trust in his abilities and do as much as he can each day, focusing on getting his individual tasks done as well as possible.

GETTING INTO THE RIGHT BUSINESS

One of the most important factors in determining your level of success in any field is the degree to which you have gained the skills necessary for that field.

No one can make it as a music educator if they lack strong personal musical ability. No one can make it very far in the mechanical professions unless they have extraordinary mechanical ability. No one can make it in business unless they have a natural knack for negotiation and sales. Yet fully formed skills in your chosen field are no guarantee of financial success.

True musical genius can not always buy success. However, some artists never rise beyond poverty despite their gifts. Blacksmiths and carpenters, for example, often have superior mechanical skills but seldom prosper financially. There are also successful businesspeople who are adept at dealing with unsuccessful customers.

The various abilities are resources. Having high-quality equipment is crucial, but so is knowing how to put it to good use. Each decent piece of furniture may be crafted by a single guy using just a saw, a square, and a plane. Another person may use the same resources to try to replicate the product, but the result would be a failure. However, he lacks the skill necessary to make effective use of high-quality equipment.

Each of your mental abilities is a tool you will need to do the labor that will lead to financial success. If you choose a field that requires skills you already possess, you will have a better chance of succeeding.

Your greatest chance for success is in the line of work that makes the most efficient use of your most developed skills and aptitudes—the field to which you are most "best fitted." Yet, there are caveats to this claim as well. No one should assume that he is destined for a certain profession because of the abilities he was born with.

Even if you do not naturally possess the skills necessary to succeed in a certain field, you may always learn them and utilize them to your advantage. In other words, you will not be able to depend on the tools you were born with and will have to build your own as you go. When your skills and abilities are already established, it is much simpler to achieve success in a certain field. Nonetheless, you may be successful in any line of work since you have at least a little bit of skill in every area.

If you focus on your strengths, you will be more successful at building wealth. Yet, if you follow your passions, you will find the greatest success and happiness in your pursuit of wealth.

Enjoying life is acting on your own desires. There is no use in existing if we are forced to do something we despise and prevent ourselves from doing the things we like. And you know without a doubt that you have the strength inside you to accomplish your goals because you want to.

What we want is a sign of our might.

Motivated by a need to express and develop one's strength, musical pursuits are a powerful pursuit. Making new mechanical gadgets is a kind of self-expression and growth that is motivated by a need for control.

There can be no motivation to accomplish something if one lacks the ability to do it, whether that ability is now there or not. If you really want to achieve something, it is evidence that you have the power to do it; all you have to do is learn how to use it effectively.

If you have a choice between two businesses, choose the one in which you have the most developed skills. But if you have a burning interest in a certain career path, make that your ultimate objective.

Since freedom of choice allows you to pursue whichever interests or profession brings you the greatest joy, you should do so.

You should not undertake work that you do not like unless it is a necessary step in the direction of the task you would rather be doing.

Because of the errors you made in the past, you may be stuck in a job or working conditions that you despise for a while. Yet you may make the task more bearable if you remember that it is getting you closer to your dream job.

Do not rush into switching careers just because you fear you are not in the correct one. Business or social transformation is best accomplished via expansion.

If the chance presents itself, and you believe, after giving it some thought, that it is the correct chance, do not be frightened to make a quick and extreme shift. Nonetheless, you should never take rash or drastic measures if you are unsure of their efficacy.

On the level of imagination, time stands still.

As well as, chances are abundant.

As you remove yourself from a competitive frame of mind, you will realize there is no need to ever rush into anything. In other words, you have a 100% chance of becoming the first person to accomplish your goal. Plenty to go around. If the one you want is already taken, keep walking; you will find a better option soon enough. In other words, you have plenty of time. Do nothing hasty when unsure. Consider your vision again, and you will renew your hope and resolve. Gratitude should be cultivated regardless of the circumstances, especially during periods of uncertainty.

Spending a day or two meditating on the picture of what you desire and offering heartfelt appreciation for what you are obtaining will put your mind into such a close connection with the Infinite that you will not err when you take action.

There is a brain out there that knows all there is to know. Moreover, if you have a heart full of appreciation, you may join forces with this state of mind via your faith and your desire to succeed in life.

Acting hurriedly, out of fear, hesitation, or forgetting the appropriate motive—more life for all and less for none—are all common causes of error.

The more you stick to the plan, the more chances you will have to succeed. You will need to remain rock-steady in your convictions and focus and to have a respectful dialogue with the Ultimate Power.

Take each day as it comes, and do the best you can without panicking or rushing. Travel as quickly as possible without ever being in a rush.

Keep in mind that the minute you start to rush, you switch roles from creator to competitor. You find yourself back in the previous plane.

Stop what you are doing if you feel the want to rush. Focus on a mental picture of the outcome you want, and start practicing gratitude. Incorporating an attitude of thankfulness into your daily life is a certain way to boost your conviction and revitalize your drive.

THE IMPRESSION OF AN INCREASE

Whether you decide to switch careers or not, you still need to focus your current efforts on the work you are doing.

The manner you go about your day-to-day job might pave the road for you to enter the industry of your choice.

Furthermore, whether your line of work requires you to interact with customers face-to-face, over the phone, or in writing, your efforts should be focused on giving off an appearance of growth.

Every single human being always seeks growth. A need for greater expression arises from inside them, driven by the shapeless intellect that they are.

All living things have an innate need to expand. In a sense, it may be seen as the universe's underlying drive. All of humanity's endeavors are driven by a need for progress. To put it simply, people want more of everything: what they eat and wear and live in; what they know and enjoy; what gives their lives meaning and purpose; of what they may learn and experience.

The pressure to improve one's situation is something that all living things must do. When reproduction stops, decay and death follow quickly.

Everyone knows this deep inside, which is why there is always a want for expansion. Jesus explains this principle of unending growth in the story of the talents. It is only the winners who keep any of the money they make. "From him who hath not shall be taken away even that which he hath."

The typical ambition to get more riches is neither bad nor morally objectionable. The simple want for a better quality of life. Moreover, everyone is naturally drawn to a person who can provide them with greater material comforts; this is a basic human need.

By sticking to the sure path, as shown above, you not only benefit from it but also spread it to everyone you interact with. You are the source of growth for the whole world.

You should be confident in this, and you should reassure everyone you meet of it. Put the notion of growth into anything you are doing, even if it is as simple as selling a bar of candy to a tiny kid, and make it a point to leave the consumer impressed by the thought.

Do all you can to give the appearance that you are a progressive guy who helps others who work with your progress in their own careers and lives. Spread the idea of growth among the individuals you encounter in your social life.

You might give off this appearance by always acting in accordance with the conviction that you are advancing toward greater success. Carry out your daily activities with the belief that you are an improving personality and that you are progressing with everyone you come in contact with. Believe that you are enriching yourself and the world at large through your actions.

Do not speak excessively or gloat about your achievements. The faithful never engage in boasting.

It is safe to assume that behind every arrogant outward appearance lurks a timid, fearful individual. Let your faith guide your actions and see how things turn out. Make it clear with your every move, word, and glance that you know you are going to be wealthy and that you know you are rich. There will be no need for words to express how you feel. People will be drawn to you because they will experience a boost in confidence whenever you are in the room.

You need to make a strong enough impression on them that they see only the upside in working with you. If you are going to take money from them, at least offer them something of more worth in return.

Take genuine delight in your work and promote it to the public; it is the best approach to ensure a steady stream of satisfied customers. Wherever there is growth, people will flock, and because the Supreme Power seeks expansion in all areas and is aware of all things, unknown individuals will soon be making their way toward you. You will be astounded by the sudden growth of your company and the unexpected good fortune that follows. You will have the option of making more substantial investments, gaining more benefits, and progressing into a more agreeable line of work.

Yet, while you go about all this, it is crucial that you keep your goals and your faith in mind at all times.

To continue my warning about your motivations, I must warn you about the subtle allure of seeking authority over others.

Nothing is more satisfying to a mind that is still developing than being dominant over others. The ambition to govern for one's own pleasure has been the root of all evil throughout history.

For endless eons, lords and monarchs have shed untold amounts of blood in their quest to increase their own power and territory. They have not been trying to save the world's population by any means but rather to advance their own political status.

The driving force behind modern-day industry and commerce remains the same. Each new round of the insane battle for dominance over others involves the same mobilization of monetary armies and the resulting destruction of millions of lives and countless hearts. Much like political monarchs, commercial tyrants are driven by an insatiable ego and a craving for absolute control.

The thirst for power was the driving force of the wicked world that Jesus came to destroy. See how Matthew 23 depicts the Pharisees' desire to be called "master," to sit in the high places, to dominate others, and to impose burdens on the backs of the less fortunate.

Take note of how he contrasts this desire for power with the brotherly concern for the benefit of everyone that he exhorts his followers to adopt.

Watch out for the need to want to be in charge, to get to the top, to be seen as better than others, and to show off lavishly.

The competitive mind is not a creative mind since it is focused on winning at the expense of others. Rule over others is not required to achieve mastery over your surroundings and your fate. Indeed, when you join the global war for power, you give up on your surroundings and destiny, and making money becomes a game of chance and speculation.

Competing thoughts may be dangerous. The late Golden Rule Jones's favorite saying sums up the notion of creative action perfectly: "What I want for myself, I want for everybody."

MAN ON THE GO

Everything I discussed in the last chapter is applicable to the working professional, the wage earner, and the merchant.

No matter what field you are in, success and wealth will come your way if you can help others improve their quality of life and help them see the value of this improvement. The physician who sees himself as a great and successful healer and works with faith and purpose toward the full fulfillment of that vision will come into such intimate contact with the Infinite that he will achieve remarkable achievement. His practice will attract a large number of patients.

The medical professional is in a unique position to put the ideas presented in this book into practice. The healing principle is universal and accessible to practitioners of every school. Thus it makes no difference which one he practices. If a medical student or practitioner can maintain a positive self-image and practice the laws of faith, purpose, and thankfulness, he or she will be able to successfully treat any patient who responds to treatment.

There is a great need for ministers who can impart the genuine science of abundant living to their congregations. A preacher who has mastered the science of becoming wealthy, as well as the related sciences of health, greatness, and romantic success, will never be short of followers. In other words, this is the gospel the world desperately needs. Using this method will result in a longer lifespan. Many will be receptive to hearing it, and those who deliver it will get enthusiastic backing.

A demonstration of the science of life from the pulpit is now required. To be effective, preachers must be able to not only instruct their congregations but also serve as living examples. To learn how to become prosperous, healthy, wonderful, and well-liked, we need the guidance of a preacher who already exemplifies these qualities. When that day comes, he will find a large and devoted fan base waiting for him.

Equally important is a teacher who can impart to their students the hope and meaning that come from living a life on the cutting edge. Such individuals will always have work available. And educators who share this conviction and sense of mission may pass it on to their students. If it is something they often do, they feel obligated to share it with the person asking for it.

What holds true for professors, ministers, and doctors holds true for attorneys, dentists, real estate agents, and insurance agents, too.

My method of combining mental and physical effort is foolproof. This is an impossible situation. Every person who diligently, persistently, and to the letter follows these guidelines will become wealthy. A mathematical proof of its validity may be found for the law of the growth of life, just as it can for the law of gravity. Making money is a quantifiable science.

This will also be true for the salary earner. Do not give up hope of ever becoming wealthy just because you are currently employed in a job with no obvious path to growth, low pay, and expensive living expenses. Create a firm mental image of your goals and go out to achieve them.

Put forth as much effort as possible every day, and make sure every task you do is completed well. Infuse your actions with the energy of success and the will to accumulate wealth. But do not do it only to impress your boss or higher-ups with the expectation that they will notice your hard work and promote you. It is quite doubtful that they will accomplish that.

An employee's worth is highest when he or she just does his or her job well and is content with it. When it comes to the company's bottom line, promoting him is not a priority. There, he has greater value than here.

To go ahead, you need more than just to be too big for your britches. The individual who is sure to rise to the top is the one who is too large for his current role and who understands exactly what it is that he wants to become and is fully committed to making that goal a reality.

Do not overextend yourself in an effort to get your employer's approval by remaining in your current position. Consider it an investment in your future success, and do it with that in mind. Have your mind and heart set on success even when you are not on the clock. Keep it in such a manner that everyone you come into touch with, from your boss to your coworkers to your new friends, can sense the strength of your resolve. Always remember why you are fighting and never give up, and everyone around you will feel a sense of growth and development emanating from you. It will not take long until you draw the attention of others, and if you can not rise in your current position, you will find a new one that suits you better.

As a man moves forward in accordance with the law, he is always rewarded by a higher authority. If you conduct yourself in a certain manner, God will have no choice but to assist you. Doing so is necessary if he is to aid himself. Not even the state of the economy or the job market can derail your ambitions. If you can not make it big in corporate America, maybe you can work on a 10-acre farm. And if you start going in the right direction, you will get away from the multinational corporations and onto the farm or anywhere else you want to go.

A business would be in serious trouble if even a fraction of its workforce following a given path. For survival, it would need to provide its employees with additional options. There should be no obligation to labor for low compensation. As long as there are individuals who are either too stupid to learn about the science of being wealthy or too intellectually lazy to put it into practice, the corporation will be able to maintain people in seemingly hopeless situations.

The moment you commit to this style of thinking and doing, your faith and resolve will enable you to see any chance to improve your situation.

These openings will present themselves rapidly because the Ultimate Power, active everywhere and always on your side, will direct them in your direction.

Do not sit about and wait for a chance to make your dreams come true. Whenever you are ever faced with a chance to grow and develop into a better version of yourself, you should follow that urge and seize it. If successful, this will be the gateway to much larger prospects in the future.

Someone living a progressive lifestyle will never be at a loss for options.

Everything happens for a reason, and it is written into the fabric of the universe that man's progress and happiness are intertwined. He will undoubtedly become wealthy if he adopts the appropriate mindset and conducts himself accordingly. To that end, I urge all working adults to read this book thoroughly before embarking on the path of action I outline in it. It can not possibly fail.

SOME CAUTIONS

The concept that there is a precise science behind achieving financial success is seen with derision by a great number of people. Because they are under the belief that there is a finite amount of wealth available, they will urge that changes need to be made to social and governmental institutions before a significant number of people may gain riches.

Nevertheless, this is not the case.

It is true that the majority are kept in poverty by the governments that are in place today; however, this is because the masses do not think and behave in a particular way. If people started acting in accordance with my recommendations, there would be no way to stop them, not even with the help of governments or industrial systems. To allow this forward migration, all of the systems would need to undergo some kind of modification.

Nothing could possibly prohibit people from becoming wealthy if they had the mind of progress and the faith that they could do so; otherwise, they would remain poor.

Riches can be made by anybody, anywhere, at any time, as long as they follow a specific path to success, regardless of the political system in place. And when a sizeable number of people in any government's population do this, it will lead the system to change in a way that will make it possible for others to follow in their footsteps.

The more males there are who are successful on the competitive plane, the more difficult it is for those who are not. On the creative level, the more people who succeed in becoming wealthy, the better it is for everyone else.

Only by encouraging a large number of people to become wealthy through the use of the scientific technique outlined in this book would it be possible to save the economy of the masses and bring about social justice.

These individuals will lead others in the right direction and instill in them a desire for real life, along with the conviction that such a life is attainable and the determination to pursue it.

Yet, for the time being, it is sufficient to be aware that neither the government that you live under nor the system of industry, whether it be capitalistic or competitive, can prevent you from being wealthy. You will become a citizen of a different kingdom once you enter the creative plane of thinking because you will have risen beyond all of these things and entered a higher dimension.

But keep in mind that your thought process needs to remain on the creative plane. You are under no circumstances to operate in a competitive manner or consider the supply to be constrained in any way.

If you see that you are slipping back into old habits of thinking, you must immediately correct yourself. This is because when you are in the mind of competition, you no longer have the cooperation of the Highest Power.

You should not spend any time anticipating how you will respond to any emergencies that may occur in the future. It is not appropriate for you to worry about urgent matters that may come in the future; rather, you should focus on completing the tasks assigned to you for today with complete and total success. You are able to tend to their needs when they present themselves.

Do not worry about how you will overcome challenges that may appear on the horizon of your business; instead, focus on running your company effectively. Disregard these queries unless it is completely obvious to you that you need to make a change to your plan right now in order to escape these obstructions.

It does not matter how large an obstacle looks from afar; if you keep moving in the same direction, it will vanish as you get closer to it, or you will discover a method to go over, through, or around it. This is true even if the obstacle seems insurmountable from afar.

If a person is determined to amass wealth using only scientific methods, there is no way that they can be thwarted by any conceivable confluence of events. There is no way that a man or woman who abides by the law can fail to become wealthy any more than it is possible to multiply two and two and not obtain four.

Do not let yourself become concerned by ruminating on potential catastrophes, impediments, panics, or unpleasant combinations of events. There is sufficient time to deal with such things as they arise in the here and now while they are immediately in front of you. You will discover that despite its appearance, every obstacle comes with the resources necessary to overcome it.

Watch how you use your words. Never speak in a demoralizing or discouraging manner about yourself, your affairs, or anything else, no matter the topic.

Never concede that there is a prospect of failing, nor should you ever speak in a way that implies there is a chance of failing.

Never refer to the current era as challenging or the current state of the business climate as uncertain. It is possible that individuals on competing aircraft are facing challenging times and uncertain commercial prospects, but that will not ever be the case for you. You have the power to create whatever it is that you desire, and you are not bound by fear.

When other people are going through difficult times and have a poor business, you will find the most opportunity for yourself.

Teach yourself to think of and to look at the world as something that is becoming - something that is growing - and to consider apparent evil as being just that which is undeveloped. Train yourself to think of and to look upon the world as something that is becoming - something that is developing. Always frame your comments in terms of moving forward. To act in any other way would be to contradict your faith, and to contradict your faith would be to abandon it.

Never give yourself permission to feel disheartened. You might anticipate having something in your possession at a particular time, yet end up not having it at that time instead. This will give the impression of being unsuccessful. Yet, if you remain steadfast in your faith, you will discover that the apparent failure is merely an appearance.

Continue in a particular direction, and even if you do not obtain that thing, you will receive something so much greater that you will realize that the apparent failure was really a stepping stone on the route to a significant triumph.

A student of the science of getting rich had his heart set on forming a particular business partnership that, at the time, appeared to him to be highly desired. Nevertheless, things did not go as planned. It took him a few weeks of hard labor to make it happen. When it got down to the wire, the thing failed in a manner that was completely incomprehensible. It seemed as if an unseen entity had been plotting against him in the background all along. He did not feel any sense of discontent. On the other hand, he praised God that his wish had been denied, and he continued on with a grateful attitude. In a few weeks, he was presented with an opportunity that was substantially greater than the first transaction. If he had known about the second chance, he would never have gone through with the first one. He realized that a mind that knew more than he did have protected him from squandering the opportunity to achieve the larger good by being entangled with the lesser.

If you preserve your faith, remain committed to your mission, maintain an attitude of appreciation, and strive to accomplish as much as you possibly can on a daily basis, then every apparent setback will work out for the best in the end.

It is because you have not asked enough questions that you end up making mistakes. Keep going, and something far better will come your way than what you were looking for in the first place. Always keep this in mind.

You will not be unsuccessful simply because you do not possess the requisite talent to do what it is that you want to accomplish. If you continue in the manner in which I have directed you, you will eventually cultivate all of the talents that are required for carrying out your work.

The topic of the science behind developing talent is not going to be covered in this book because it is outside the scope of what is covered here. On the other hand, the method of becoming wealthy is just as certain and uncomplicated.

You should not be hesitant or wavering because you are afraid of failing because you do not have enough ability when you get to the stage where you are supposed to fail. Continue in the same direction, and when you reach that point, the ability will be made available to you there. You have access to the same pool of talent that enabled somebody with little formal education, like Abraham Lincoln, to do more in government than has ever been done by a single person. You have the ability to use the thinking mind to help you meet the duties that have been placed on your shoulders. Continue with complete confidence.

Read this book carefully. Take it with you wherever you go and make it your constant companion until you have learned all of the concepts that it contains. You will do well to give up most recreations and pleasures while you are getting firmly established in this faith. Moreover, you will do well to keep away from areas where competing views are presented in lectures or sermons. Do not read any literature that is negative or that contradicts itself. It is recommended that you read relatively little outside of the authors specified in the introduction. Invest the majority of your time in your leisure activities in reading this book, practicing gratitude, and reflecting on your vision. It explains all you need to know to become wealthy, including the science behind it. In addition, the following chapter will provide a concise summary of all the important points.

CONCLUSION

There is a thinking stuff from which all things are produced and which, in its natural state, permeates, penetrates, and fills the interspaces of the world. All things are composed of this thinking stuff.

The manifestation of the item that is envisaged by thought in this substance is produced by the thought itself.

A person is able to shape things in his thoughts, and then, by impressing those thoughts upon formless substance, he can bring about the creation of the object that he is thinking about.

In order to accomplish this, a person's mindset needs to shift from one of competition to one of creativity. Otherwise, he will not be able to be in harmony with the formless mind, which is always competitive in spirit but always creative.

One way for a person to achieve complete harmony with the formless substance is to cultivate a robust and heartfelt sense of gratitude for the blessings that are bestowed upon him by the formless substance. A person's mind can become unified with the thinking mind via the practice of gratitude, allowing the individual's thoughts to be received by the formless essence. One of the few ways for a person to remain on the creative plane is for them to unite themselves with formless intelligence by cultivating a profound and unending sense of gratitude.

A person needs to create a distinct mental image of the things he wants to have, achieve, or become before he can go forward with those goals. Moreover, he is required to keep this mental image in the forefront of his mind while he expresses his profound gratitude to the Ultimate Power for fulfilling all of his wishes. The individual who wants to amass a lot of wealth should devote most of his spare time to reflecting on his goals and offering heartfelt gratitude for the fact that those goals are becoming a reality for him. It is impossible to place an excessive amount of emphasis on the significance of regularly reflecting on the mental image in conjunction with unshakeable faith and heartfelt thanks. This is the process by which the formless substance receives an impression, and this is also the process by which the creative forces are started in motion.

Creative energy operates through the pre-existing systems of the natural world, as well as the existing systems of the industrial and social order. All of the things that are depicted in his mental image will undoubtedly be made available to the individual who faithfully follows my instructions and who does not waver in their trust. What he desires will be delivered to him via the tried and true channels of commercial and trade activity.

A person has to be doing something in order to receive what is rightfully his when it is prepared to be given to him. He needs to do more than just maintain his current position. It is imperative that he keeps in mind the goal, which is to amass wealth through the execution of his mental vision. He is required to accomplish everything that can be done on a daily basis, making sure to carry out each task in an effective manner. To ensure that each transaction results in an increase in life, he is required to provide each individual with a use value that is greater than the monetary value he is paid. In addition to this, he needs to keep the notion of progressing in his mind at all times in order to give the appearance that things are getting better to everyone he interacts with.

Those individuals, whether male or female, who put the above recommendations into effect will unquestionably attain financial success. And the wealth that comes to them will be directly proportional to the clarity of their vision, the firmness of their purpose, the consistency of their faith, and the extent of their appreciation for what they have been given.

DISCLAIMER

This book is for entertainment purposes only. Readers acknowledge that the author does not render legal, financial, medical, or professional advice. The content within this book has been derived from various sources. Please consult a licensed professional before attempting any techniques outlined in this book.

By reading this document, the reader agrees that under no circumstances is the author responsible for any direct or indirect losses incurred as a result of the use of the information contained within this document, including but not limited to errors, omissions, or inaccuracies. Adherence to all applicable laws and regulations, including international, federal, state, and local governing professional licensing, business practices, advertising, and all other jurisdictions, is the sole responsibility of the purchaser or reader. Neither the author nor the publisher assumes any responsibility or liability whatsoever on behalf of the purchaser or reader of these materials. Any perceived slight of any individual or organization is purely unintentional.

ABOUT THE AUTHOR

Born into an upper-middle-class family as the only child, she was raised in an environment that beautifully blended the natural world, courtesy of her father, a forest and RNB contractor, and the nurturing care of her homemaker mother.

Her professional journey began as a stock market trader, but she soon delved into the intriguing realm of healing by exploring the law of attraction. Guided by luminaries like Louise Hay and mentored by esteemed figures such as Guru D.S. Sastri, Ms. Swathirekha, Mitesh Khatri, and Mr. Sashi sir, she achieved the distinguished title of a Level 4 healer in Pranic Healing.

Drawing from a rich tapestry of teachings, including Reiki Grand Mastry under the guidance of Mrs. Swarnamala and NLP from Vikram Dhar, she blossomed into a seasoned life coach. This transformative journey was further enriched by the experience of marrying at the tender age of 18 and welcoming two beautiful boys into her life.

When the formidable challenges of the COVID-19 pandemic struck, wreaking havoc on her husband's business and finances, she found solace in applying her accumulated knowledge in real-life situations. It was amidst this turmoil that the idea for this book was conceived.

The book ***"Master Your Wealth"*** is a testament to her resilience, a chronicle of the profound insights gained through her personal odyssey. Through this book, she generously shares a mosaic of wisdom, offering readers a chance to glean from her hard-earned experiences.

MAY I ASK YOU A FAVOR?

At the outset, I want to give you a big thanks for reading this book. You could have chosen any other book, but you took mine, and I appreciate this. I hope you have at least a few actionable insights that will positively impact your daily life.

Can I ask for 30 seconds more of your time?

I'd love it if you could leave a review of the book. That will help me grow my readership by encouraging folks to take a chance on my books.

Keeping it straight - *reviews are the lifeblood of any author.*

It will take less than a minute of your time but will tremendously help me reach out to more people. **Kindly provide your review at the store you bought this book from.** And I'd love to see your review. Thanks for your support.

* 9 7 9 8 8 6 5 0 1 9 2 0 6 *